BOYS KNOW IT ALL

Wise Thoughts and Wacky Ideas
From Guys Like You

D1414991

WRITTEN BY BOYS JUST LIKE YOU!

Compiled by Michelle Roehm

BEYOND
WORDS
Publishing
I N C

Published by
Beyond Words Publishing, Inc.
20827 NW Cornell Road, Suite 500
Hillsboro, Oregon 97124
503-531-8700/1-800-284-9673
www.beyondword.com

The information contained in this book is intended to be educational and not for diagnosis, prescription, or treatment of mental and/or physical health disorders, whatsoever. This information should not replace competent medical and/or psychological care. The authors and publisher are in no way liable for any use or misuse of the information.

ISBN: 1-885223-87-7

Editors: Michelle Roehm, Todd Claus, and Marianne Monson-Burton

Cover Design: Marci Doane
Interior Design: Heather Serena Speight
Proofreader: Heath Lynn Silberfeld/Enough Said
Printed in the United States of America
Distributed to the book trade by Publishers Group West

Library of Congress Cataloging-in-Publication Data

Boys know it all : wise thoughts and wacky ideas from guys just like
    you / written by boys from across America ; compiled by Michelle
    Roehm.
        p.   cm.
        "Kids books by kids, 3."
        Summary: More than thirty boys from around the country write on
    issues ranging from sibling problems and using computers, to how to
    talk to girls.
    ISBN 1-885223-87-0
        1. Boys--Psychology--Juvenile literature. 2. Boys--Conduct
    of life--Juvenile literature. 3. Boys--Health and hygiene--Juvenile
    literature. 4. Boys--Life skills guides--Juvenile literature.
    5. Interpersonal relations--Juvenile literature.   [1. Boys-
    -Psychology. 2. Conduct of life. 3. Boys--Health and hygiene.
    4. Life skills. 5. Interpersonal relations. 6. Children's
    writings.] I. Roehm, Michelle   1968-
    HQ775.B64   1998
    305.23—dc21   98-7590
                                              CIP
                                              AC

The corporate mission of Beyond Words Publishing, Inc: *Inspire To Integrity*

A THANK YOU FROM THE EDITOR

"While girls' horizons have been expanding, boys' have narrowed, confined to rigid ideas of acceptable male behavior."

—*Newsweek*, May 11, 1998

In 1997 we published a book called *Girls Know Best*, which was written entirely by girls. The girls of America loved it, but the boys were less than thrilled. They said to us, "Hey! What about the guys? Where's our book? We've got a lot to say, too!" So we launched the "Boy Writer Contest," asking boys ages six to sixteen to send in their best nonfiction ideas. I have to admit, we were a little worried that we would get nothing but football tips and Nintendo secrets. Man, were we wrong!

The "Boy Writer Contest" ran in magazines and newspapers across the country, and we did get a few sports entries. But we got even more entries from boys who were concerned about how the world tells them what they should be when they grow up, what hobbies they should enjoy, and who their heroes should be. It took us months to read all the amazing stories and ideas we received, but we finally chose twenty of our favorite guy chapters. There are the expected chapters on catching slimy creatures and doing martial arts, but there are also chapters on doing your own thing in spite of peer pressure, cooking for guys, and even creating your own comics.

The thirty-two boy authors have been a blast to work with (way more fun than grown-ups). They've learned about deadlines, editing, and proofreading. I've learned the best way to catch bullfrogs, how to handle a dis, and all about the "boys' movement." They get the first thanks for making my job fun.

Choosing the winners and editing the chapters has been a HUGE job. I was very lucky to have a great group of people helping me make this the coolest boy book ever. I couldn't have done it without Todd Claus, Gove

DePuy, Marianne Monson-Burton, and Amanda Hornby. Without their excitement and hard work, this book never would have happened.

Thank you also to the parents, families, friends, and teachers of the boy writers included in *Boys Know It All*. Your support and encouragement have helped these young authors achieve their dreams. And a special thanks to all the boys who entered the contest. The ideas we received were truly inspiring. Each of you has the ability to change the world and make your dreams come true, so don't give up. Enter another "Boy Writer Contest" (see back of book) and send your writing to other publications (see Justin Bailey's chapter "Do the 'Write' Thing" for ideas).

I hope *Boys Know It All* shows the world that there is a new breed of boys out there—brave guys who are tired of their limited choices and are exploring new roles and options. If the girls have "girl power," boys too are trying out their own "boy power." These boy authors have shown me that being different and achieving your dreams takes a strong belief in yourself.

And if they can do it, so can you!

—Michelle Roehm

TABLE OF CONTENTS

DO YOUR OWN THING!

Carl Massey, age 14

✂ **Hobbies:** tap dancing, playing sports with my family, drawing, playing on computers, watching movies, talking on the phone ✎ **Favorite class:** P.E. and science
✐ **Favorite author:** Roald Dahl ☺ **Pet peeve:** when someone asks me the same question over and over
♬ **Hero:** my dad ❀ **Dream:** to be a Jefferson Dancer and to become famous all around the world for my dancing.

Doing your own thing is a very important topic to me. You see, I am a tap dancer with my brothers and sisters, in a group called The Hot Shot Tap Dancers. I spend a lot of time dancing and practicing, and I get made fun of for it. Some kids think it's uncool for a guy to dance. But guess what? I don't care what other people think or say about me and my dancing. I dance because it is so much fun and I love it. Plus I know that I can have a great career if I stick with it. I want to share my experience with other boys to show them that it's okay to dance or do anything else that's "different." It's cooler to do your own thing than to do what other people think you should do.

Life as a Dancer

First I'll tell you a little about what it's like to be a dancer. These are the questions that people always ask me when our dance group is out performing:

Q: Why did you decide to be a dancer?
A: I saw some people dancing on TV when I was a little kid. It looked exciting, so I asked my dad if I could try it. He said "sure," and I've been doing it

ever since. I love it because it takes energy and excitement, it makes other people happy, and it's great exercise.

Q: Is it hard to dance?
A: It is hard in the beginning when you start out. But if you enjoy it, it becomes easier. Dancing takes time and hard work. It doesn't come to you the very first time you put dance shoes on your feet, but eventually it does come.

Q: How much do you have to practice?
A: I practice about ten to fifteen hours per week, depending on what dance shows or competitions we have coming up.

Q: Do your feet hurt from all that dancing?
A: Oh yeah! My feet are always sore. But lately we've started soaking our feet in saltwater for fifteen minutes every day. This really toughens them up.

Q: How long does it take to become a really good dancer?
A: It depends on how much capability you have for learning and getting the teachings down. Also, it takes a lot of discipline to practice on your own, take lessons, and listen to your teacher. You have to really want to do it. If it's someone else's idea, then you'll never stick with it.

Q: How is your dancing different from studio dancing?
A: Our dancing is from the soul and not what we just learned to do from a teacher. We choreograph many of our numbers and do a lot of improvisation (make stuff up on the spot). Some studio dancers never learn to do that—they just learn the steps. When you dance from your soul, your body takes over and you have more fun doing it.

Q: Do kids tease you because you don't do a "regular" sport?

A: I do play "regular" sports, it's just that I don't plan to make a career out of them. I played soccer for five years. I even wanted to play football for a while, but I was too busy with my dancing. Sometimes kids still tease me for dancing because it's different from what they do.

Q: Are there other dancers who inspired you by "doing their own thing," even though it wasn't "cool" at the time?

A: Some of my heroes are the famous tap dancers like Sammy Davis Jr., Buster Brown, and Savion Glover (the creator of the very cool Broadway show "Bring in Da Noise, Bring in Da Funk"). These guys all stuck with dancing until they were so good that no one could tease them anymore. They helped make dancing cool.

Q: Wouldn't you rather play with your friends than practice dancing?

A: Of course. But I also know that I have to practice to be good at it. It's the same with anything—if you want to be a great football player, you have to practice. If you want to be a great guitar player, you have to practice. I want to be a great dancer, so I practice and sometimes I have to sacrifice fun with my friends. For me it's worth it. Dancing pays off in so many ways. You can get trophies, you can get scholarships, and in some cases you can get paid! Believe it or not, dancing is a good way to make a living. And if you do become famous, you can make a lot of money. Plus, I love to do it.

Q: Is dancing worth the sacrifices and the teasing?

A: Yes. There are lots of reasons I stick with dancing even though it takes work and sometimes people make fun of me: It's really fun, I like the benefits, I like the publicity, I like traveling to different places and meeting new people. I also like to make people happy by entertaining them. And I like earning my own money doing something I love.

Why You Should Do Your Own Thing

I am here to say that if you like to do artistic things, or anything that's "different," then you should do what makes you feel good. Don't listen to people who say bad things about what you want to do. There is a lot of satisfaction that comes from doing your own thing.

For one thing, if you're a guy who does anything artistic you just might get more credit for doing these things. Since not very many guys do it, there's less competition for you. For example, there are not a lot of male dancers, so my dancing makes it easier for me to get good parts in plays and other events that require a male dancer.

Lots of guys dream of becoming professional athletes. They should realize that the competition for this is much harder. They're not likely to make it to the big time because there are a lot of really good people in this world who can play their sport. On the other hand, I am already making money by performing, and if I want to continue dancing I will make even more money at it.

If you want to, you too may be able to make a career out of what you enjoy, like I have. Male dancers are in big demand all over the world. My goal is to be a Jefferson Dancer (a very competitive high school dance team) and then to become famous all around the world as an entertainer. Fame is only one of the many good things that will happen to me in my career as a dancer.

Believe it or not, being a good dancer also makes you very popular with the ladies. Just ask some older women if they would like to date a man who is a good dancer. Girls and women think that a guy who can dance is very romantic and charming.

Doing something different might lead to other benefits that most guys don't get. I have had many opportunities because of dancing. I have traveled all over the United States and have met many famous people. I have strong self-esteem and a lot of pride in myself because of what I do. I know I am good at dancing and that makes me feel good about myself in general.

Don't Let Teasing Stop You from Doing Your Own Thing

It's not just guy dancers who get teased. All guys get teased for something at some time in their lives. Some get teased for not playing the right sports. Some get teased for singing in choir . . . for being poor . . . for not wearing the right clothes . . . for talking to the "wrong" kids . . . or just for being different. The list goes on and on. I've thought a lot about why some kids tease me about my dancing, and here's why I think they do it:

☞ They can't do what I do.

☞ They don't see other guys doing it, so it must not be a "guy thing."

☞ They are jealous or insecure.

So, why do people tease you? Is it really because there's something wrong with you? Or is it because there is something wrong with the person teasing you? Here are some reasons I think kids tease other kids:

☞ They're jealous.

☞ They're mean.

☞ They're rude and don't have any manners.

☞ The other kids aren't like them, they're different.

☞ They're very insecure and it makes them feel like they're a "higher rank" than the other kids if they can tease them.

I don't think it's a good idea for guys to try to change who they are or give up on their dreams just because someone else has a problem and feels the need to tease them. It's not worth it!

But What Can I Do if I Get Teased?

As I said, people have made fun of me before. Some try to impersonate me and at the same time insult me. Sometimes it hurts my feelings, but I always keep in mind that I love what I do. Dancing is fun. Anything you like to do should be fun and you should be proud of it—not ashamed.

Everyone deals with teasing in their own way. I think that letting it get to you is just what teasers want, so I don't give them the satisfaction. Here's what I do:

☞ Ignore them. It's pretty hard to keep teasing someone who doesn't give them any reaction. They stop pretty quick.

☞ Confront them and ask, "Why are you saying that? Why is it such a big deal to you that I'm doing what I want to do? Don't you have something better to do?"

☞ Try to get them into it with you. Sometimes kids are just afraid to be different and it makes them feel better to tease you for your bravery. If you offer to teach them or get them involved, that may be all the invitation they need to get over their fear and give it a try.

☞ Tell them about all the benefits of what you do. I tell them about the money I make, the travel I get to do, the excitement of being on stage in front of fans, and of course the fame!

I hope one of these responses works for you and helps you do what you love without worrying about what others will say.

If you think that what you are doing is fun, then you should stick with it, no matter what other people say or do. Don't let anyone stop you from doing what you like. If you like it and you have fun doing it, you shouldn't listen to people who try to put you down and bring you down to their level. Later, when you get older and those kids don't matter to you anymore, you will only regret that you caved in and didn't do what you wanted to do—that you didn't act like who you really are. If I can do it, so can you. Be brave—do your own thing!

Carl doing his own thing.

CATCHING CREEPY CREATURES

Roland Howard III, age 11

✂ **Hobbies:** catching frogs and turtles, playing Nintendo 64, in-line skating, target shooting, playing football, and fishing ☒ **Favorite class:** history 📖 **Favorite book:** *Hatchet* ☹ **Pet peeve:** when my sister comes in my room without asking 🏳 **Hero:** my family ✴ **Dream:** to go to college and have plenty of money

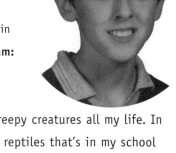

I've loved frogs, turtles, lizards and other creepy creatures all my life. In fact, I've read *every* book about amphibians and reptiles that's in my school library. My favorite, *Reptiles and Amphibians of the World*, has photographs of over 200 species. I know them all by name and where they come from.

I really love catching creepy creatures because you can do it just about anywhere and there isn't anybody to tell you how to do it, when to do it, or where to do it. You just go outside, lift up a few rocks and logs, and you've got yourself something creepy. Guys in my neighborhood are amazed at how I'm able to catch so many frogs and turtles. They want to hold my frogs and turtles. They beg me to give them one or to show them where they can find their own. Usually, I keep my creatures and secrets to myself because I don't want other kids to take too many or to neglect what they find.

Now I've decided it's time to "let the turtle out of the bag" and pass on my top-secret techniques. I know you'll have fun catching creepy creatures, and I hope you will listen to my instructions for releasing whatever you catch back to its original pond or lake! That way there will always be enough creepy creatures out there for all of us to enjoy. Remember: These are wild creatures that deserve to stay that way!

Creature-Catching Gear

There are certain things you will need to catch frogs and other creepy creatures. Most equipment can be found at thrift stores or yard sales, as well as the stores indicated. Here's what you'll need:

Equipment you need for small frogs, toads, lizards, and snakes:

- A small, goldfish-size net, available at most pet stores.
- A large jar and lid (with air holes punched in it) with a mini-habitat (mud, water, leaves, etc.) inside.

Equipment you need for large bullfrogs and turtles:

- A large trout-size, round, mesh net, available at most sporting goods stores.
- A deep bucket complete with mini-habitat. Turtles need enough water to cover their bodies. Be sure to get the water from the pond they were found in.
- Enough mesh netting to cover the bucket. It's usually sold by the yard and can be found in most hardware stores. Large rubber bands, Velcro, or string keeps it in place.
- Newspapers to cover the floor of your parents' car (if you're traveling by car).

Optional equipment:

- A fish tank is a good idea if you plan to catch and release creatures on a regular basis. A five-gallon tank is best, plus enough mesh netting to cover the top of the tank.
- Rubber boots or waders (thigh-high are best) can be used to go directly into ponds. These are used by people who fish in streams and can be bought in sporting goods stores.
- Books about the kinds of creatures you want to catch and learn about are fun. They'll help you with care and feeding.

Where to Find Creatures

Frogs & toads on dry land:

Tree frogs and very large bullfrogs can be found on the banks of ponds and lakes. They tend to hang out in the yellow grassy brush that is growing near the bank or in nearby green bushes. To find them, simply spread apart the brush while carefully looking for movement.

> **How to tell if it's a toad:** Toads have super bumpy skin and live only on land. Toads are found in the wooded areas under logs and leaves. When the sprinklers are on, they can be found in the damp grass eating bugs.

Frogs & toads in the water:

Most people don't see frogs like I do. I know just what to look for. Most ponds and lakes are full of frogs. Your best bet is to find a pond or lake that has lots of bushes, grass, and, best of all, green moss. Reptiles and amphibians love it because they can hide in it and it keeps them cool. Look near the edge of the water, where frogs usually sit. Start by lifting up rocks and dead logs. Look on rocks and in the mud.

> **Roland:** *A few years ago, I found a huge bullfrog that was as round as a football. He was just sitting in the brush near the water's edge. My mom freaked when she saw him, he was so big. I placed my large net over him and tried to hold it down with both my hands, but this frog's legs were so strong that when he jumped, he pushed me off and hopped away!*

Turtles:

Turtles like the same water conditions as frogs. If you can find green moss, you'll find a turtle. You can spot them by their noses sticking out of the water. In the summer, they sit on logs or hang out on the banks of the ponds. At times, logs are so crowded with turtles that the creatures sit on top of each other. In Oregon, I usually find one or two per pond. In Idaho, it seems there are hundreds in every pond.

Lizards, Salamanders, and Newts:

Salamanders and newts like to hang out where it's cool and muddy, so look under your garden hose or in the dark and muddy areas around your house. Dark, wooded areas are full of salamanders and newts. Look under rocks, logs, and piles of leaves. You'll have better luck when it's raining.

> **Roland:** *My family and I discovered an awesome spot to catch rough-skinned newts and Northwestern salamanders. We went to a nature reserve right in the middle of our town. The woods are super thick and when we first arrived we didn't find anything. But when we got away from the path and wandered into a muddy area with few plants and lots of dried-up logs, we were surrounded by newts and lizards. Everywhere we looked we could see newts and lizards. My mom kept saying, "There's one! There's another!" It gave my mom the creeps so bad that she screamed and ran back to the trail. When she screams I know I've hit the jackpot!*

Snakes:

Snakes like the same conditions as newts and salamanders. Look in dark, wooded areas under logs and in piles of leaves.

> **Roland:** *On another trip to the nature reserve we brought my friend Zack. Once again, we were in a muddy, flat area with few bushes and plenty of logs when my mom saw garter snakes everywhere. She screamed extra loud and seemed to run in mid-air. Jackpot! Zack is really into snakes, so he caught four that looked pretty creepy slithering in the jar.*

Finding Woods and Ponds in Your Neighborhood

Even if you live in a city, you'd be amazed at how many places there are for you to look for creatures. Call the Audubon Society, 4-H clubs, or your town's parks and recreation offices. Get a map of your town or city. I got a map once from the parks and recreation department that showed all the neighborhood boundaries. But it *also* showed every small creek in town.

When you're out driving around with your parents (or riding your bike) look for ponds off to the side. I usually look for ponds that aren't too deep and are easy to get to. If you learn to spot plants that grow near ponds, you'll be able to find ponds all over the place. You'll be surprised how many there are in your very own neighborhood that you didn't even know about!

10 Tips for Catching Creepy Creatures

For each creature there are specific tips and secrets that will help you find and catch them. Here is a general technique that will help you to catch *any* creepy creature.

1. Go to their habitat, as I described above.
2. Walk super slow and quiet because if you scare them they'll take off and hide. So don't bring people who like to talk a lot! As you walk, move aside bushes and turn over logs and rocks.
3. Watch for any sudden movements and listen for creature noises.
4. When you see something that's moving fast, quickly place your hand or a net over it before it can get away.
5. If it's moving slowly or is stopped, you slow or stop too.
6. Approach it from behind or at an angle.
7. If you move slowly, the creature will forget you're there and will relax.
8. Then, slowly, inch by inch, extend your hand or net out until it's over the creature.
9. Then swoop down and grab or net it—*gently*! You don't want to squish it.

10. Put the creature in your bucket and cover the top with netting so it can't escape until you're ready to let it go.

Water Stalking

Water Warning: If you decide to go in the water, be sure you know how to swim AND be sure you have an adult with you all the time. Obviously, there is some risk of drowning when you do anything in the water.

Level 1 Water Stalking:

The first couple of times you'll probably want to capture the creatures from the shallow bank while wearing rubber boots or old sneakers. Keep your eyes peeled for bulging eyes, noses, ripples or bubbles in the water, movements, or things that look alive.

Level 2 Water Stalking:

After you've been catching creatures for a while, you will want to wade into the water to get them. You may want boots or waders, so that you stay dry. Once you are willing to go in the water, you can catch a whole lot more. You'll be able to sneak up on stuff and have a lot more fun. In Idaho, I didn't even wear waders—I just went in the water without them. I was usually up to my neck in slime. My family even called me "Swamp Boy"!

How to Snatch Them Up

The Basic Net Technique:

Sneak up on them from behind, or diagonally from the side. If you're in shallow water, place the net over the top of the creature. If you're in deep water, scoop up the creature from underneath. It's much easier this way. Once the creature is in the net, gently secure it with your hands to place it in your container. Your catch's legs will move a lot (especially frogs), but whatever you do, don't drop them.

The Bare-Handed Technique:

Slowly sneak up from behind. When you get super close, quickly grab the creature with two hands and be ready to hang on. If it slips away, quickly reach down into the murky water and feel around. It's best to keep your hands cupped together to create a sort of trap. If you move fast, you'll have a good chance of finding it in the muck.

Extra Catching Tricks and Tips for . . .

Frogs:

With bigger frogs (by big, I mean BIG! football-size frogs) you've got to move in on them quickly, because the larger they are the better their hearing is.

Toads:

Toad Caution #1: Toads have a gland behind their eyes that has poison in it. If you get this poison in your mouth or eyes, you could get sick. So, be sure to wash your hands after touching a toad.

Toad Caution #2: When toads get scared, they pee—a lot!— another good reason to wash your hands.

Snakes:

Snake Warning #1: Some snakes can be dangerous. If you plan on catching them, you definitely have to get a book that shows the different species of snakes. A book will help you to tell which snakes are poisonous and better left alone.

Snake Warning #2: Most snakes stink like dirty socks. They also like to pee on you. Wash your hands after touching them.

When grabbing a snake, grab it by the back of the head and hang on gently but firmly because it will wiggle a lot. Place it in the jar *tail first*.

Turtles:

When you see a turtle, slowly go around to the back of him so he can't see you. Then sneak up, stoop down, and slowly put your hand out. When you're close enough to grab him, move fast. Hang on gently but firmly by cupping your fingers around the edge of his shell. Avoid his mouth because turtles bite.

If you know how to swim, get in the water and grab the turtle from underneath. If it dives down, just feel around in the water and you may be able to still get it.

Taking Care of Creatures

Sometimes I'll keep a creature that I catch for a few days. I'll set up a nice habitat for it at my house, and then I can watch it and study it up close. But within a week or so I release it back to where I caught it. Otherwise it will die because it is a wild creature and is not used to living in a cage or fish tank. If you want a pet that you can keep forever, you should go to a pet shop and get one.

Creating Mini-Habitats for . . .

Frogs, lizards, and snakes:

These creatures need about two inches of mud, some rocks, and some branches with leaves on them. They also need a shallow, sturdy bowl for drinking. *Make sure the water doesn't have chlorine in it.* Chlorine can kill small creatures, and most tap water has chlorine in it. If you plan to use tap water, get rid of the chlorine before you use it. Chlorine remover is sold in pet stores and most grocery stores. Follow the directions for making one gallon, and use that for your creature's water supply. Or, you can use pond water or rain water instead.

> **Roland:** *Right now I have two tree frogs that I got at a pet store. Recently, they mated and had babies. So now I have fifteen little froggies that are only as big as Lincoln's head on a penny.*

Turtles:

Turtles need enough water to cover their bodies and to moisturize their eyes. But they also need to get out of the water to dry off their shells. So fill the tank halfway with water, then pile rocks high enough so the turtle can get partially out of the water. This water will get dirty fast, so plan on releasing the turtle after a few days, change the water, or buy a water filter.

Sunlight

Full spectrum light (sunlight) is important, so keep your creature near a softly lit window. However, hot, direct sunlight can bake your creature and kill it, so be careful to never place it near a bright window or outside in the direct sun. An artificial, full-spectrum light can be bought in most pet stores.

Creature Food

Frogs eat crickets. Lizards eat crickets and bloodworms. Turtles eat goldfish, crickets, and turtle pellets sold at pet stores. Snakes eat a variety of things from insects to goldfish. The creature books and/or someone who works at a pet store can tell you more details on what to feed your creature. You can buy the bugs at a pet store or catch them yourself.

NEVER Do This:

- **Never put creatures in your pocket**. A long time ago, when I first started catching creatures and didn't know anything, I caught four frogs and put them in my pocket. Then I totally forgot about them. Later that day, I remembered and tried to pull them out, but they were all dead. All I could feel was FROG JELLY! You think that's gross, huh? Well, what was *really* gross was that I couldn't even pull them out because their tongues were stuck to my pocket! I had to cut them off with scissors. I still feel terrible about that experience because it was a waste of life. I should have let them go.

- **Don't be greedy!** When I was younger and lacked a conscience, I brought home over twenty turtles. I put them all in a rubber raft in the backyard and left. When I returned, there were turtles running everywhere! Lots of them had escaped onto the road in front of my house and got smashed by huge trucks. I felt awful and will never do that again!

- **Never hurt the creatures you catch!** In case the stories from my past don't convince you that you shouldn't ever hurt creatures because they are so cool and you will feel bad about it later, here's another reason. Most of us know that many animal species are extinct or in danger of going extinct. Human pollution is causing deformities and hurting animal eggs and babies. Our planet can't stand to lose any more amazing creatures. I hope that when you practice my techniques, you will remember to treat the creatures carefully and with respect and to quickly release them back into their original homes. Believe it or not, our planet depends upon their survival. And besides that, they are really cool.

- **Don't keep wild creatures as pets.** Sometimes I'll keep a creature that I catch for a little while. I'll set up a nice habitat for it at my house, so I can watch it and study it up close. But within a week or so I release it back to where I caught it. From my past experience, I've learned two things about keeping wild creatures as pets. 1) They will die because they grew up in the wild and aren't used to living in a cage. 2) Eventually I get tired of taking care of them every single day and want to put them back anyway. By that time, they may be too sick to live in the wild, or they may have forgotten how to catch their own food because I've been feeding them, etc. It's better just to return them after a few days of checking them out. If you want a pet that you can keep forever, go to a pet shop and get one.

- **Don't set creatures free inside your house.** If you do, one of these things will likely happen: 1) You'll lose it. 2) Another one of your pets will attack and kill it. 3) It'll get trapped behind something and will die and stink up your whole house. 4) Your parents will find out and kill you!

> **Roland:** *When my dad was little, he caught several coffee cans full of leopard frogs. For some crazy reason he thought it would be fun to set the frogs free inside the house. My grandma was hysterical when she found them, and my dad got grounded—not a good idea!*

- **Don't set free any creatures you buy at pet stores.** If you have a frog that you bought at a pet shop and it's from China, it might cause other native species (creatures that are originally from your area) to decrease. When bullfrogs were released outside of their native habitat, they ate other frog species, birds, snakes, salamanders, newts, toads, and even bats. One of the reasons you shouldn't let pet store species go is because you never know what might happen. You might really mess up the nature where you live.

Roland's Top 10 Favorite Creepy Creatures

1. **Leopard Frog**—These North American frogs were the ones always dissected by high school biology classes, but they used so many that now these frogs are rare.

2. **Bullfrog**—These huge North American frogs eat smaller frogs, turtles, snakes, and even birds!

3. **Pixie Frog**—Even though they're called pixies, these frogs are even bigger than bullfrogs. They're also called African bullfrogs because that's where they're from.

4. **Alligator Snapping Turtle**—This North American turtle can weigh more than 300 pounds, can bite a broomstick in half, and has a pink lure on its tongue to catch fish with.

5. **Rattlesnake**—Most people don't know that rattlesnakes, which are found all over America, are very shy and usually only bite you if you surprise them or go near their nests.

6. **Spiny Red Newt**—If you pick up this Asian amphibian, it will arch its back and poisonous spines from its ribs will stick you. Yikes!

7. **Fire Salamander**—This cool salamander has black and yellow stripes that look like flames, and it lives in Europe, Africa, and Asia.

8. **Painted Turtle**—This beautiful North American turtle has a shell that looks painted in yellow, black, red, green, and orange.

9. **Spiny Softshell Turtle**—This guy, who lives in America, can stretch his neck out longer than his body and has a very nasty bite.

10. **Poison Arrow Dart Frog**—These Central American frogs have the most poisonous venom known to humans.

Roland's Creepy Creature Factoids

1. Some frogs can lay more than 10,000 eggs. Out of those, only 400 to 600 will survive to become frogs.
2. The largest frog in the world, the Goliath frog, is about as big as a baby deer and weighs eight to nine pounds—probably more than you weighed when you were born!
3. It takes six years for bullfrog tadpoles to lose their tails and become real frogs.
4. Frogs will eat themselves to death if they get too much food, so never feed them more than a few crickets at a time.
5. Horned frogs can bite and draw blood.
6. The largest freshwater turtle can weigh over 300 pounds.
7. A fully grown boa constrictor can strangle and eat a crocodile.
8. Some turtles lay their eggs in alligator nests for protection. When the baby turtles hatch, they have to scramble for their lives to escape the hungry momma alligator.
9. On some beaches, thousands of turtles will come to lay their eggs. They lay literally *millions* of eggs on these beaches.
10. Tiger salamanders can eat frogs, lizards, and turtles. They even burrow into the ground to chase moles!

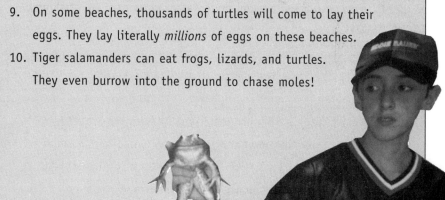

Roland with his latest catch.

THE SCOOP ON GIRLS

Doug Kuykendoll, age 13

✦ **Hobbies:** golf, basketball, bowling, playing video games

✎ **Favorite class:** pre-algebra 📖 **Favorite book:** *Let's Get Invisible*

☹ **Pet peeve:** fingernails on a chalkboard 🎗 **Hero:** Michael Jordan

✤ **Dream:** to be a professional golfer

Brian Norris, age 13

✦ **Hobbies:** sports ✎ **Favorite class:** math 📖 **Favorite book:** *Robinson Crusoe* ☹ **Pet peeve:** cole slaw 🎗 **Hero:** Reggie Miller ✤ **Dream:** to play for the Chicago Bulls

Arnie Sullivan III, age 13

✦ **Hobbies:** basketball, bowling, golf, riding dirt bikes, shopping, getting girlfriends ✎ **Favorite class:** pre-algebra 📖 **Favorite book:** *The Stand* 🎗 **Hero:** Michael Jordan ✤ **Dream:** to be a professional basketball player

We chose to write about the opposite sex and how to get along with them because we feel that most guys have no clue how to act around girls. Some guys act very immature and do all the WRONG things. Some guys are totally shy and get too nervous to do anything. And some guys are just plain rude and inconsiderate with girls. Let's face it: Guys out there need help.

So, what do girls want from us? What are they looking for in a guy? How can we get them to like us? These are the questions most guys want answers to. We asked ourselves, "Selves, what's the best way to get the *real scoop* on what girls think and what they are looking for?" The answer is, of course, girls themselves. So we gave all the girls we know (and some we don't know) a survey with all the questions guys want to know. Here are their answers . . . the inside scoop . . . top secret information . . . the G-Files . . . don't show this to anyone!

THE OFFICIAL
"WHAT ARE GIRLS LOOKING FOR?"
SURVEY

Traits Girls Look for in Potential Boyfriends

We asked girls what the most important and least important personality traits they looked for in guys were.

Here is what girls are **looking for in a guy** they want to date:

1. You should be **nice**.
2. You should be **honest** (tied with "nice" for first place).
3. You should be **sensitive**.

And here is what **girls don't care about at all:**

1. You don't need to be **rich**.
2. You don't need to be **artistic**.
3. You don't need to be **athletic**.

So, while it's really important to be nice, honest, and sensitive to the needs of the girl of your dreams, guys, it's totally unimportant to be rich, super creative, or athletic! So put away the cleats, the fancy car, and the poetry. Just be yourself!

How to Tell a Girl You Like Her

If you like her, these girls said the best way to let her know is to:

1. **call her** on the phone.
2. **write her** a note.
3. **tell her friends**, so they can tell her.

Top 10 Things to NEVER Do
Around the Girl of Your Dreams

Here's the list of what girls said we should never do in front of a girl if we want her to like us:

1. **Never be sexist!**

   "Don't order my food for me, make all the decisions, be overprotective, or show me off." —Amy Chapman

   "Don't say things like 'hubba-hubba' or be a brute." —Emily Bachelder

   "Don't snap my bra!" —Anonymous

   "Don't ever try to do things to me without my permission."
   —Desirei Calloway

2. **Never be mean!**

   "Don't even think about insulting or embarrassing me or my friends."
   —Anita Bishop

3. **Never pick your nose** . . . *"or my nose!"*—Amy Chapman

4. **Never burp, spit, or fart!** DUH!

5. **Never *"show off, brag, or stare at another girl."***—Taylor & Hannah

   "You can't impress me by fighting."—Desirei Calloway

6. **Never *"stare at my chest."***—Nicole Breazeale

7. **Never use curse words!**

   "Don't cuss around my family (suck up instead)." —Anonymous

8. **Never be annoying!**

   "Don't yell in front of everyone, 'I like you!' and then point to me."
   —Anonymous

   "Don't breathe loudly and be really nervous."—Jody Bates

   "Don't ask questions about things that aren't any of your business."
   —Emily Rossi

9. **Never smoke!**

10. **Never *"pretend you're so cool."***—Emily Bachelder

The Best Places to Take a Girl on a Date

It's our opinion that a guy shouldn't date until he's ready for it. Some people feel ready later than others, so take your time and don't rush into it just because other guys are dating or have girlfriends. Wait till you're ready.

When you are ready to start dating, here are the places that girls said they'd like to go. Overwhelmingly, the best place to take a girl is to **the movies**, and **the mall** is a distant second. But as one girl told us, it doesn't matter much where you go, as long as it's "fun and not boring." On the other hand, Amber Johnston said she preferred going someplace quiet like "an overlook or a park."

The girls listed some other favorite date spots:

1. a restaurant or café

2. the zoo

3. a picnic

4. a fair or carnival

5. a walk or a hike

The Best Gifts to Give a Girl

Give your parents back their ATM card! You're not going to need it to impress your favorite girl. The girls we surveyed said what matters isn't expensive gifts but your honesty, reliability, respect, and friendship. While a number of girls said they think flowers, cards, candy, or inexpensive jewelry are nice, none think the way to a girl's heart is through your wallet.

Listen to what a few girls think is important:

"Gifts from the heart."—Anonymous

"Words, a kind note."—Justine Blount

"The simple gift of him loving me."—Thomisa Cassidy

"Being himself, and really being caring."—Anonymous

"You can't buy her love, you just have to be yourself."—Anita Bishop

The Big Secret About Girls

We asked the girls to tell us the one secret that we guys really don't know about them. Here's what they said:

- ♥   Girls are smarter than boys think they are.
- ♥   Girls are not wimps!
- ♥   *"Girls love sincere attention, and lots of it!"*—Nicole Breazeale

If there are any more secrets about girls that guys are clueless about, Allison Singhoffer says she's *"Not telling!"*

First Impressions

We asked the girls if there was some kind of "pick-up line" that would get their attention when a guy first meets a girl. The overwhelming response was "No, pick-up lines don't work." Just be yourself and say "hello." Don't try to be too cool!

"No pick-up lines, PLEASE! Just introduce yourself."—Nicole Breazeale

Getting Your Parents to Drive You Without Ruining Your Date

For those of us who don't have our own licenses yet, going on a date can be torture if our parents have to drive. So, how can you get your parents to drive and still have a good date? The girls had a lot of great suggestions.

1) *Don't* ask your parents to drive you. You and your date can take the bus together or walk.

2) Ask an older brother or sister to drive (if you have one)

3) The most common and best advice was to talk to your parents about your concerns. Be honest. Let them know what is happening and how important the date is to you. And once they agree to drive you, ask them nicely to keep their distance.

Holding Hands or Arm Around?

The ballots are in and 85% of the girls in the survey said they would rather hold hands than have the boy put their arm around her. Carla Risner said holding hands is "more romantic," and a couple other girls said that holding hands is better because it will make the girl feel more comfortable and secure than will putting your arm around her.

The Final Step—Asking Her to Be Your Girlfriend

Now that you know the inside scoop from the girls—what to do, where to take her, what she's looking for, how to show her how you feel—you may have a special someone that you'd like to ask to be your girlfriend. Here's our advice for the best way to start:

♥ Get to know her as a friend first. That way you can get comfortable with her and get to know her better.

♥ After you've gotten to know her and you're sure you really like her, ask her if she wants to go out somewhere with you. Most of the time you will get a better response if you ask her face-to-face. Only cowards ask someone else to do it for them. If you have someone else ask her, she might think you're afraid to do it yourself and will most likely say "no."

♥ If you decide to ask her face-to-face, approach her when she's alone. Say something like, "We've been friends a long time and I was wondering if you want to go somewhere or do something with me sometime?"

♥ If she says "yes," ask her where she'd like to go. Make sure you go to the place alone together. If you go with friends, then you'll never be able to ask her if she likes you too.

♥ Once you're out on the date and alone together, you can bring up the scary question: "Will you go out with me?" "Will you be my girlfriend?" or whatever guys at your school say. By that time it shouldn't be so hard to ask her because you're already friends, you're comfortable with her, and now she even agreed to go out with you alone. Your chances are good.

♥ If she says "yes," then you can start calling her and talking to her a lot.

♥ If she says "no," then ask her if you can still be friends. If you're nice about it, there should be no problem being friends again and you haven't lost anything.

So, that's the inside scoop. Those are the answers right from the mouths of the mystery—girls! Now you know what they want, what they don't want, and how to treat them. Have no fear, just be yourself. That's what they want, after all!

GOOD LUCK!!!

JUST JOKING

WISE-CRACKS TO MAKE YOUR BUDDIES LAUGH

Dillon Sprague, age 13

✂ **Hobbies:** soccer, collecting comic books and cards ✂ **Favorite class:** tech ed 📖 **Favorite book:** *Deathwalk* ☹ **Pet peeve:** green beans and when people snort when they laugh ♬ **Hero:** Jerry Lewis ✱ **Dream:** to make one of the best movies in the world

Terry Chan, age 14

✂ **Hobbies:** baseball, hockey, tennis, and playing video games ✂ **Favorite class:** P.E. ✎ **Favorite author:** R.L. Stine ☹ **Pet peeve:** getting blamed for things I didn't do ♬ **Hero:** Cleveland Indians' second baseman, Joey Cora, #28 ✱ **Dream:** to be a major league baseball player and/or to join the air force

Do you love to crack your class up? Do you make people shoot milk out their noses during lunch? Do you laugh at your own stupid jokes louder than anyone else? If so, then you are just like us—class clowns. We love telling jokes, especially with a bunch of guys. Here are some of our favorites to crack up you and your friends.

Q: What do you get if you cross a wake-up call with a chicken?
A: An alarm cluck!

Q: How do angels answer the phone?
A: "Halo?"

Q: Why couldn't the skunk use the phone?
A: Because it was out of odor.

Q: Why did the turtle cross the road?

A: Because he wanted to go to the Shell station.

Joke: A guy buys a horse from a farmer who tells him, "To make the horse go, you whistle. To make him stop, you say 'whoa.'" The guy rides until he sees a cliff ahead. He starts yelling, "Stop, horse, stop!!!" as he gets closer and closer to the cliff. At the last second he remembers and says, "Whoa!" The horse stops right at the edge of the cliff. The guy whistles in relief and the horse jumps off the cliff.

Q: Why is a seagull called a seagull?

A: Because if it lived by the bay it would be called a bagel.

Q: What's a ghost's favorite berry?

A: Boo-berry

Joke: A robber breaks into a house and is walking down a dark hallway when he hears a mysterious voice say, "Ralph is watching you." He turns around and sees a parrot. "Are you Ralph?" the robber asks the parrot. The parrot shakes his head no. "Then what is your name?" he asks. The parrot replies, "My name is Lionel." The robber laughs and says, "What kind of a weirdo would name his parrot 'Lionel'?" "The same weirdo who named his pitbull 'Ralph'," squawks the parrot.

Q: What does a volcano sneeze sound like?

A: "Ash-oo!"

Q: What do you call a skeleton at the dog pound?

A: A treat.

Joke: Four people are flying in a plane—the pilot, the president of the United States, the Pope, and a young kid. The plane runs out of gas and is going down. The pilot grabs one of the three parachutes and jumps. The president says, "I have to lead the country," grabs the second bag, and jumps. The Pope tells the kid, "You take the last parachute. You're young and have a long life ahead of you." "That's OK," says the kid, "there are still two parachutes left." "How?" asks the surprised Pope. "The President took my backpack," says the kid.

Q: What did Tarzan say when he saw the elephants coming over the hill?
A: Here come the elephants.

Q: What did Tarzan say when he saw the elephants wearing sunglasses coming over the hill?
A: Nothing. He didn't recognize them.

Joke: A waiter is so sure that he's the strongest man around that he offers $1,000 to anyone who can squeeze just one drop of juice from a lemon that he squeezes first. Lots of people try (weight lifters, longshoremen, etc.) but none are able to win the money. One day a scrawny little man wearing thick glasses and a polyester suit comes into the restaurant. In a tiny voice, he says, "I'll try the bet!" After the laughter dies down, the waiter grabs a lemon and squeezes away until only the wrinkled remains are left. He hands this to the little man, and as the crowd watches in amazement, he clenches his fist around the lemon, and . . . SIX drops of lemon juice fall out. The crowd cheers and the waiter pays the $1,000 bet. He asks the mysterious man, "What do you do for a living? Are you a lumberjack, a weight lifter, or what?" The man replies, "No, I work for the IRS."

Q: What does an elephant wear for a toupée?
A: A sheep.

Q: What does the grape say when you step on it?
A: He makes a little whine.

Joke: A woman at a gas station sees a flying saucer approaching. As it lands she sees "U.F.O." written on it. When the alien comes out she asks it, "Does 'U.F.O.' stand for 'Unidentified Flying Object'?" The alien replies, "No, it stands for 'Unleaded Fuel Only.' Fill 'er up!"

Q: What did the strawberry say when he got into trouble?
A: "Well, this is a fine jam I'm in!"

Q: What's yellow and goes, "Slam, slam, slam, slam"?
A: A four-door banana.

Q: What's yellow and goes "Slam, slam, slam, slam, bang"?
A: A four-door banana with a flat.

Q: What did the old chimney say to the younger chimney?
A: You're too young to smoke.

Joke: A boy is home alone when he gets an unexpected call. The creepy voice on the phone says, "I'm the viper. I'll see you in an hour." The boy gets scared but decides to ignore the call. Half an hour later he gets another call from the same man saying he'll be there shortly. The boy gets another call fifteen minutes later and this time the voice says, "I'll be at your door in five minutes." The boy locks his door and starts to get very scared. Just then the doorbell rings. The boy is shaking with fear but decides to look through the door's peephole. Through the peephole he sees a short stubby man, so he opens the door. The man says to him, "I'm the vindow viper and I vant to vash your vindows."

Q: What is red and goes up and down and up and down?
A: A tomato in an elevator.

Q: What is green and swims at the bottom of the sea?
A: Moby Pickle

Q: Why didn't the skeleton cross the road?

A: Because he didn't have the guts.

Joke: *Bad news:* A man jumped out of a plane. *Good news:* He had a parachute. *Bad news:* It didn't work. *Good News:* There was a haystack down below. *Bad news:* There was a pitchfork in the haystack. *Good news:* He missed the pitchfork. *Bad news:* He missed the haystack.

DOING THE TEAM THING
THE SOUL OF SPORTS

Scott Lawrence, age 11

✈ **Hobbies:** watching jets at air shows with my dad, soccer, street hockey, and playing the piano

🖌 **Favorite class:** science 📖 **Favorite book:** *The Magnificent Mummy Maker* ☺ **Pet peeve:** when I have to clean my room and would rather be playing 🎹 **Hero:** my dad ✿ **Dream:** to be a top-gun fighter pilot in the navy

I chose this topic because I really like sports. I've been playing sports like t-ball, basketball, and soccer since I was four years old and I've been lucky to have great coaches teaching me about true sportsmanship. Hopefully my advice will help you understand the soul of sports, make joining teams easier and playing more fun, and help improve your game.

Why Be a Jock?

I think that the best reason to get into sports is because sports are fun! Here are some of the reasons I love playing sports:

Make new friends. Sports are a great way to make friends. You make friends with kids on your team, and you can also make friends with kids on other teams.

Travel the world. Playing sports gives you a chance to travel and meet kids from other schools, other districts, and other towns. You may go to school with those kids later, or they might live near you but go to a different school. Playing sports with them helps create new friendships.

Fun with the family. Sometimes games and tournaments are far away. Traveling to them is a great chance to get away, see the sights, and have fun with your friends and family. We've had some great family outings on these sports trips.

Fun for everyone. Getting involved in sports is fun for more than just us kids. Even adults have fun. My parents meet lots of other parents and make lots of friends at our practices and games. My dad wasn't totally excited about attending a class to be a ref for my sister's soccer team, but when he did he learned a lot about the game and ended up really enjoying himself.

What Does It Take?

There are all sorts of skills to learn for every sport: how to pass; how to score; the rules; the tricks. But the most important things to learn in sports aren't the rules, or tricks, or moves. To truly understand the soul of sports, you need to learn the deeper lessons. You need to learn what it takes to be a great athlete—heart, teamwork, support, preparation, commitment. Do you have what it takes?

Heart and Soul

The first thing to know about playing sports is that it takes up valuable time—your time (when you could just be relaxing), your teammates' time, your parents' time, and your coach's time. So, don't join a sport if you're just going to waste everybody's time by goofing around during practice. Make the most of practice time by paying attention and trying your best. One season in soccer my team lost almost every single game we played because all we ever did at practices was fool around. It was no fun! You may be the worst player, with no sports experience at all, but you'll still win if you put in the effort during practices and games. Give it your heart and soul and you will always be a winner.

Check Your Attitude

The fun of sports depends on the attitudes of the kids playing together. If people have bad attitudes and always yell at each other and get into arguments, then it isn't fun for anyone. Players with bad attitudes also get carded often and thrown out of games, and that's definitely not fun. If you have a good attitude, then practices and games will be fun for everyone.

Get Some Respect

A big part of playing sports is learning to be responsible. If you want your coach and teammates to respect you, then you need to respect them. It's your responsibility to make it to all of the games and practices. If there's a real emergency and you have to miss a practice or a game, be sure to call the coach as soon as possible so he knows how many players will be there and what to do without you. Don't ever think you are so good you don't need to practice. Not even Michael Jordan is that good.

Can You Juggle?

Sometimes, when you start playing a sport, it can be hard juggling all your responsibilities: practice, homework, family, friends. Try to get your homework done before practice or games (at lunch, right after school, and even on the bus going to games). That way, when you get home you can relax, hang out with your family, and talk to your friends without having to worry about the homework due the next day. After practice or a game you're often too tired to concentrate anyway. And if you start turning homework in late or not studying for tests, your parents will find out and you may have to quit the team. In my house the rule is "Get your homework done or the sports go." Wanting to play sports actually helps me get better grades, because it's a privilege I want to keep.

Total Teamwork

The word "team" means a group of people organized to work together. For me, "TEAM" stands for "Together Everyone Achieves More." Learning about teamwork when you're young is good because when you get older and get a job, teamwork will be important. In a job, you're part of a team that has to get a job done. You'll have an easier time if you already know how to work with a team. You might not like somebody you work with, but you are still on a team together and you need to get along so the job gets finished. The boss is like the coach of the team, making sure you work together to do the best job.

The Blame Game

I remember a soccer game in which we were beating the other team. Instead of working harder to win, the other team started blaming their goalie for letting balls in the goal. This didn't help their game at all. The goalie got so upset and frustrated that we scored even more goals on him. Those players didn't understand that they are part of a team and they are all responsible for how they play. If the defense does a good job, the goalie doesn't have to work so hard. Everyone contributes to how the game is going, not just one person.

When teammates screw up or play badly, chances are they already know and are beating themselves up for it. If you get angry and yell at them, they'll just feel worse than they already do. That attitude puts more pressure on them, which they really don't need from their own teammates. When you put negative pressure on people, they usually tense up, get very nervous, and play even worse. That's bad for the whole team!

If your teammate's in a slump, he needs your support and positive comments to pull out of it. Say things like, "Don't worry, you'll get it next time, " or "Hey, so-and-so needs some support. Let's pull together, team!" Encourage your team in every situation, especially the bad ones. If you win, that's great, but if you don't, that's okay too. You tried your best, worked as a team, and had fun. That's what it's all about.

Be Prepared

To be at your very best during a game, there are some key things you need to do to prepare your body.

Stay in shape. It's important to stay healthy and strong. Practices and working out will keep you in shape and strengthen your skills.

Get enough sleep. If you don't get enough sleep before a game, you will be tired and weak the next day and won't play your best. A good night's sleep will help you feel alert and strong.

Eat a good breakfast. Playing sports on an empty stomach will really hurt your game. Believe it or not, a great thing to eat for breakfast is chicken noodle soup. It warms you up, is nutritious, and gives you lots of energy without giving you that stuffed feeling in your stomach.

Stretch and warm up your muscles. Get to your game early so you can warm up and stretch before the game. That way you won't get a cramp or injury. Without good stretching before a game, you can easily cramp up in the beginning of the game and end up sitting on the sidelines with an ice pack. Most game injuries happen when players don't stretch out enough.

Being a Good Sport

Being a good sport means acting like a gentleman. Your behavior during a game reflects on your entire team, your coach, and your parents. So remember, while you're on the field or the court, conduct yourself with dignity, respect, and maturity. Here are some easy ways to be a good sport:

Don't have a foul mouth. Some kids think it's cool to say bad words during games because they think it makes them sound tough, but all that really matters is how you play the game. One day those kids will grow up and realize how stupid they acted. If you get angry at someone, ignore them and focus on the game. If a call makes you angry, control your tongue and let your coach handle the situation. Play on and remember that you are a gentleman.

Don't play dirty. It seems like a lot of professional athletes today play dirty during games, but that doesn't mean that it's right. That's not what sports is about. While playing sports you should try to have a clean game—tripping opponents or giving them the elbow is playing dirty. It's usually when players get crazy and play dirty that people get hurt. If everybody played clean there would be less injuries. Winning by playing dirty isn't fair to anyone, but winning fairly because of your skills is great. Even if you don't win, that's okay. You played your best, you played fair, you had fun, and nobody got hurt.

Listen to your coach. My coach once told me, "No matter how big a player seems, it doesn't mean he's better than you. You all have an athlete inside your soul, but you must use your mind to bring him out." During the game, always keep one ear tuned to your coach. If he or she places you in a position that you don't like, remember that all coaches have their reasons and maybe next time he or she will let you move into a position that you like. If it really bothers you, don't whine and complain during the game—just do your best. Save your complaint for the next practice, then politely tell the coach your thoughts.

Don't let bad refs ruin your game. Sometimes referees can be frustrating. In one game a player from the other team cussed at me throughout the game and said if I didn't let him score a goal he'd beat me up. The ref totally ignored it. When I didn't let the guy score, he pushed me. When I pushed him back, we both got carded by the ref.

When I play on teams where the refs are volunteer parents, sometimes it seems like the refs favor the team their kids are on. That's annoying too, but taking out your frustrations on bad refs or on other players will do you no good. That will only get you on the ref's bad side or even get you thrown out of the game. I recommend that you talk to your coach during a break and tell him/her what's going on. Let them fix it for you. My experience has shown me that the team with the better discipline and commitment can win the game no matter how bad the ref is.

Sports Jams

When you play sports, there will always be challenging situations. Things happen that are hard to deal with and may even make you consider quitting the team. All athletes go through this. Here are some tips for recognizing these sports jams and solving them so you can stay in the game.

Coach's son on the team?

What if your coach's kid is on your team and he gets treated differently from the rest of you? Do you complain to the coach and risk getting kicked off the team? Or do you suffer through the unfair treatment? Quite a dilemma.

This actually happened to a friend of mine. He got mad because he was on a soccer team with the coach's son. The coach's son was a lazy player, fooled around at practices, but still got the best positions during games, and when he scored a goal he got all the recognition, even though he had plenty of help from the rest of the team. This unfair treatment made the whole team very angry, but no one said anything to the coach because they were afraid they'd get kicked off the team. My friend actually quit because nothing ever changed.

Before you give up, I recommend talking to an assistant coach or your parents about your concerns. If that doesn't work you may need to quit the team and join another or wait until next year. It worked out well for my friend because he started the following season with a new team and coach that he was very happy with. Sometimes you need to know when to move on.

Girls on the team?

Some guys have a hard time playing sports with girls on their team or on opposing teams. If you're one of those guys, lighten up. The old days are gone and girls can do the same things we can. There are great girl athletes and bad girl athletes, just like there are great boy athletes and bad boy athletes. It's not whether they're a boy or a girl but how they play the game, right?

I know a guy who had a bad attitude about girl athletes, and during a game he teased a girl on the opposing team. He called her names and made her really mad—he thought that because she was a girl she couldn't do anything to stop him. This boy was the goalie and toward the end of the game this girl made a breakaway and scored on him! He felt bad and stupid . . . and embarrassed. So never underestimate your teammate or opponent, whether they're a girl or not.

Who gets the goal glory?

When a player gets a goal or makes a basket, should he or she get all the recognition? Some coaches will just praise that one player. A good coach, however, will praise the whole team. After all, it's a team effort. Usually, the defense gets the ball to the offense and someone assists to the player who goes for the score. One person hardly ever scores without help. If more coaches praised the whole team, it might eliminate ball hogs. The glory should be for the whole team.

You can help show the coach and your other teammates how it's done by cheering for the players who assist in the goal and showing recognition for others on the team who contribute to the score. Eventually your team and coach will get it.

Foul coaches?

Once, when I was playing near the other team's coach, I heard him tell one of his players to try and injure me so I'd have to leave the game. If you're playing against a bad-apple coach, here's what you can do: Ignore him and his dirty tricks and play even harder to show him that you're a better sport than he is; or tell your coach about it and let him take care of it.

But what if it's *your* coach who's the problem? My friend was on a team where his coach kept him in the same position all the time and never let him play anywhere else. He hated it because he never got to learn about other sides of the game. No matter what your coach problem is, the advice to my friend should work for you: Take your coach aside before or after practice and tell him that you'd really like to try some different positions during the next game (or whatever your specific problem is). Tell him your reasons, explaining how your request will help make you a better player and more valuable to the team. Then, in the next game or practice, put your heart and soul into it. Show him that you're not just whining—you're willing to work for it.

The Hardest Lesson

One of the hardest lessons for us kids to learn is that it doesn't matter if you win or lose. It only matters if you have fun playing because that's what sports are all about—fun. You should choose a sport that you enjoy playing and just learn to have a good time. Winning isn't everything, so don't take it too seriously. It is just a game, after all.

High School Hopes?

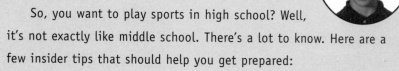

Cody Aker, age 11
❀ **Dream:** To be successful in an athletic job

John Mitchell, age 12
❀ **Dream:** To be in the NBA and to be a basketball coach

So, you want to play sports in high school? Well, it's not exactly like middle school. There's a lot to know. Here are a few insider tips that should help you get prepared:

1) You're coming in with lots of other kids, and some of them are bound to be better than you. Even if you were the best player in middle school, you might not be the best in high school. Be prepared for harder competition. Work hard in middle school and in the summers to get ready for a more difficult game.

2) When you're trying out for the team, the coaches expect a lot from you. Don't be shy—show them what you've got. Show them your very best. You won't get a second audition.

3) If you do make the high school team, you'll have to learn all the plays in a pretty short time. It may seem overwhelming at first, trying to keep up and learn. It may be possible to take play books home to study them, but also pay close attention during practice when your coach explains the plays.

4) And if you don't make the team, it's not the end of the world. You can always play for intramural, club, YMCA, or even neighborhood teams until next year's tryouts. It may take a while to achieve your goal, but don't give up. Lots of great athletes got cut from teams before making it—even Michael Jordan got cut from his high school basketball team!

Create Your Own Sports

James Dunleavy, age 10
❋ **Dream:** to play in the NBA with Jack

Jack Ward, age 10
❋ **Dream:** to play in the NBA with James

Tired of playing the same old sports? We've invented some games of our own that you can play with your friends. You can create your own sports too—it just takes a little imagination.

Table Soccer
You need: 4 to 6 players (2 to 4 on offense and 2 goalies), 2 plastic cups, 1 ball of wadded-up paper.
How to play: Tip the cups on their sides for goals. Use your fingers to pass and shoot the ball. No picking up the ball.
To win: Same as soccer, the high score wins.

Flyball Baseball
You need: 2 people, 1 tennis ball, 1 sloped garage roof.
How to play: It's simple—if you're "up to bat," throw the tennis ball onto the garage roof. If your opponent catches it when it falls back, that's one "out." You get three outs. If your opponent misses it, that's a "run." You can get ten runs per inning. There are nine innings, just like in baseball.
To win: The highest score, just like in baseball.

Football 5,000

You need: 3 or more players and a football.

How to play: The person who's "it" gets the football, calls out a number between 1,000 and 5,000, and then throws the football. The other players try to catch the football. Whoever catches it gets the number called out. With each catch, add your numbers.

To win: The first person to reach 5,000 wins and gets to be "it."

Mini-Baseball

You need: 3 players, a bat, a ball, and a glove.

How to play: One person is the pitcher, one the outfielder, and one the batter. The pitcher pitches, and if the batter hits the ball and the pitcher or outfielder catches it, or if it's a foul ball, the players rotate: pitcher goes to batter, batter goes to outfield, outfield goes to pitcher. If no one catches it, the batter stays up.

To win: No winners, just play 'til you get bored or have to leave.

CREATING YOUR OWN COMICS

Carises Horn, age 16

✂ **Hobbies:** creating comics, drawing, painting, surfing, drumming ✎ **Favorite author:** e. e. cummings ☺ **Pet peeve:** people with a "herd mentality" and people who change their look rather than thinking for themselves 📖 **Hero:** my family ❀ **Dream:** to be a writer and artist for DC Comics or Marvel

I am an American Indian and an artist by trade. I enjoy painting and working on my comic books and illustrating my dad's books (he is a writer). Art is my passion in life and my greatest gift. I've really gotten into creating comics lately and I enjoy writing and illustrating them myself. Some of you artists out there may be interested in creating your own comics too, so I thought I'd share my ideas with you.

Why I Love Creating Comics

Comics are an extension of all I like to do creatively. I look forward to sitting down whenever I can, which is usually late at night, and making my comic book series come to life in front of me. It gives me a sense of accomplishment. That is why I chose comic books as my art form.

Another reason I like comics as an art form is the joy of starting and sticking with a creative project to the end. I picture what I want to put on the paper, taking it from my mind, sending it through my hand, and putting it to the paper. At the end I have a finished comic, with characters and a story. It's a challenge to do but very rewarding.

What Tools Will You Need to Create Comics?

Pencils: I use a regular number-two pencil, but use what you like best and what works for you. Try many different kinds of pencils until you find the perfect one for you.

Erasers: If you're going to create your own comics, then good erasers are essential. If you're using a regular eraser on the top of your pencil, it will wear away before you want it to. Using the jumbo erasers you get with school packs is the best. You can also use those other kinds of jumbo erasers that you put over the tops of your regular pencil erasers. Bigger is better when it comes to erasers. You will use them a lot.

Rulers: Another tool you may need is a ruler. You can use it to create a border around your drawings, giving them the box effect used in comic books. Framing your drawings in boxes keeps your comic from looking sloppy. If you don't have a ruler, you can also use the edge of a piece of paper or an envelope as a guide when drawing the boxes. Really, you can use whatever you want, so long as it makes a straight line.

Pens: There are several pens that you're going to need. All the pens should be black, some darker than others. With different shades of black pens, you can create a faraway effect or a close-up effect if you want. You're going to want to use a fine-line or hairline pen for general use, detail, and to ink in the words and the word bubbles. You can use a larger marker-type pen for covering large areas. Trial and error is usually the best way to discover which pens you'll like the most.

Paper: Paper is the most important tool. You're going to need thick paper—but not too thick. You need to test the paper before using it. You need to make sure that the paper doesn't get eaten through by the ink and doesn't curl up and wrinkle. I don't draw normal-size comics. My comics are about twice as big. So I use larger paper, often from a sketch pad. That way, I can take the larger-size paper and fold it in half to make it like a book. The type of paper you use also depends on what kind of art you want to do. For instance, when I'm painting with watercolors, I make sure to use a paper specially made for watercolors.

Where's the Best Place to Create Art?

The place to do your creating is a place that is comfortable and relaxing for you. I create my art in my bedroom. I have a drafting table with a table lamp set up next to it so I can see what I'm doing and don't hurt my eyesight (especially late at night). Some people like a quiet, peaceful space when doing art, but I like to listen to loud music while I'm working ("rage" music is my favorite for doing my art). The place where you do your art should be your place. Create your own atmosphere for your art, because your art is you.

The most important tool you will need is your imagination. Regardless of your pencils, rulers, pens, paper, or where you choose to create or how much you practice, your imagination and creativity are the ultimate things you're going to need.

How Do I Create a Comic?

I believe that creating anything is a very personal experience and it will probably be different for everyone. Here's the process I usually go through when I create my comics. First I develop my characters. They are the most important thing and the story often comes out of developing my characters.

Next, I work on the story. Sometimes that part comes easily, based on my characters' histories and motivations, but sometimes it can be more difficult. Usually at the same time I'm working on the story, I'm also imagining the settings for the story. What kind of planet do the villains live on? Where are the battles going to be fought? What will everything look like? These are important questions that I try to figure out before I begin drawing.

Once I'm done writing and editing my story, I begin working on my rough pencil sketches. I do my comics in pencil first because pencil allows me to get a sense of what I'm doing. Plus, I can erase and change things I don't like.

Once I have my original pencil drawings finished, I'm ready to ink my creation in. Now it's time to pen it in and finalize it. This part can be a little scary because I don't want to make mistakes. But if my pencil drawings are good, there shouldn't be a problem.

Where Do I Get My Ideas?

I get ideas everywhere. I got the idea for the comic book series I'm working on when I was playing role-playing games with my brother. We were playing different characters and interacting with each other, when I thought "Hey, this could make a great story." I developed the series from there, starting with our characters, making up new characters, and then moving on to the story. Doing the book has been purely fun.

Another way I do research is by reading lots of other comics and studying how they are illustrated. I look at the artist's style, the way he or she draws an arm bending or muscles moving. I look at how the artist draws light and shadows. I also study and practice sketching the shape of the human body, which is pretty hard to do (not to mention penciling and inking it in). After I study all this research, I have a better understanding of what I'm drawing.

And it is from my dreams and my thoughts late at night, when it's quiet, that I get most of my ideas. It is then that I can imagine the strange beings that challenge my comic book heroes. I often stay up too late, half dreaming, and creating on the edge of my mind . . . .

Finding Your Own Style

Finding your own style is very important as an artist and in creating comics. Aside from my comics, I also illustrate books. I've illustrated two so far and will probably begin working on a sequel soon. I illustrated both books in a primal art style, almost like cave paintings. In this style, I try to show

the connection between the surroundings and what the characters are thinking. I also try to express what is in the heart of my characters and to reveal their feelings. I want to illustrate the spirit deep within them and to show their connection to each other and to the breath of life. These goals are all a part of my individual style.

To develop your own style, you first have to figure out who you are and what is important to you. Where are your ancestors from? What do you know about your own history? What kinds of things are important to you? What do you enjoy doing? What are your own personal beliefs about people and the world? Search for answers to these questions and then put what you find into your art—this is where you will find your own style.

The style I've used is tied to my heritage. It is similar to the old Ojibway style of art, which is my mother's tribe. But I've put my own touch on it. It's important to keep your own style when using traditional styles—but don't forget to give the older styles a try too. People say I do a good job mixing the new and old. Sometimes I agree.

Creating Something Different

I believe something different is needed in the comic book world—it's time for a change. You've got your X-men and your Superman . . . but what about something new?

Early on I noticed that there were no Native American heroes or crime fighters in any comics. Don't get me wrong: Comics today aren't bad or anything. The white and the black heroes in the other comics are fine, but what about the people who are different . . . people like me, who want more? I wanted a story and characters that went beyond this dimension. That's why I decided to create my own characters and comic series, to change all that.

To create totally different characters I had to come up with heroes and villains who really had their own unique styles—heroes who don't wear their underwear outside their bodysuits; villains who don't wear a big black cape and laugh poetically at heroes who dangle over a pot of boiling acid; stories without cheesy lines like "Holy smokes, Batman!" So, I took what I know from my own life and created characters and storylines that were completely different—something spiritual and exciting—with a lot of action-packed stuff too. And so, Dark Forces, my comic book series, was born.

Creating Characters

The first thing I do when I begin creating a comic is to develop the characters. Think about it . . . most classic comics are based on strong, unforgettable characters—Superman, Batman, Spiderman, etc. Characters are the most important thing in a comic. Here is how I created some of mine:

THE VILLAINS

Genocide: First off, this villain's name means "the systematic, planned annihilation of a racial, political, or cultural group." A perfect bad-guy name, in my mind. I wanted Genocide to be totally different from all past villains, so I couldn't just copy the regular villain formula. To create Genocide's character I took little pieces, little evil traits, from every great villain I could think of. Genocide is the blending of all villains.

Cho-Kan: I really like Jackie Chan and Bruce Lee movies. After watching many of their early films and reading a karate book and some of Lee's journals, I realized that I could make a great character from all this stuff. Not only is karate good for action, but it has a spiritual side as well. Since my comic books focus on the spiritual, as well as action, a character inspired by karate seemed perfect. I created Cho-Kan as a character that Genocide could use. Cho-Kan is a tortured spirit who misguidedly believes he is indebted to Genocide by his honor—a loyalty Genocide will use for his own purposes. Genocide and Cho-Kan represent spiritless, misguided people in my comics.

Genocide, drawn by Carises

THE HEROES:

Alex Dark Storm and John Big Bear: I got my ideas for these two heroes from the role-playing games I played with my brother. Alex Dark Storm is an Indian man who owns his own book publishing company in New York City. My brother came up with the name for Dark Storm's brother—John Big Bear. Although the heroes aren't exactly modeled off me and my brother, they are brothers and there are a few similarities.

I drew tattoos to mark the faces of Dark Storm and his brother John Big Bear. They were separated at birth and marked by the priests to let everyone know that these children were mutants. In primal cultures tattoos often signify a warrior's power.

John Big Bear and Alex Dark Storm, drawn by Carises

Cho-Kan also has tattoos for this reason, but Cho-Kan's tattoos fall like tears down his face. The tears represent centuries of pain. Like the rest of Genocide's servants, Cho-Kan did Genocide's dirty work because he was promised his freedom in return.

As you can see, your characters will come from you—who you are, what you like to do, your family history. They will come from the depths of your imagination. Just keep your mind open to them and, when they come to you, make them real.

Creating Settings and Scenes

My most recent drawing depicts a battle between Alex Dark Storm and Cho-Kan. They were brought to a planet called "Mass of the Temples"—a place where characters whose spirits are owned by others come to worship their masters. Genocide promised Cho-Kan that he would be released from his honor-bound promise to serve Genocide if he killed Dark Storm here. My drawing shows that battle, but at this point in the story you can't tell who is winning.

I created this planet as Mass of the Temples because I feel that temples are the most classic way to honor someone. I also decorated the temples with petroglyphs because I think they're cool looking and also signify the spiritual and the ancient.

In every scene I draw there is a focal point—something that the reader's eye will be drawn to. I started this drawing with Cho-Kan and Dark Storm fighting as my focal point. Once I drew the scene, I followed the story idea, picturing it in my head. I drew in strange trees and plants to fill in the places around the border. This adds characteristics to the life of the planet and gives that world definition and perception.

I spent two days and sleepless nights creating this scene.

My Final Advice

I started drawing when I was very young and I had help from my brother. Although he helped me at the beginning, in the long run I had to develop myself, just as you will have to develop yourself. Try noticing shapes, forms, the bending of objects, light, and shadow. Work at creating your own way to do these things, and as always, "practice makes perfect." Remember, whatever it is that you want to create, it will come.

In the end, the ultimate thing you must have to create your own comics (or any kind of art, for that matter) is your imagination. That's the one thing you're going to need, regardless of your pencils, rulers, pens, paper, where you draw, or how much you practice. It is only on the edge of your mind that you will find what you're looking for . . . .

SYNOPSIS OF THE DARK FORCES COMIC
by Carises Horn

Alex Dark Storm and John Big Bear are swept into a life of danger and intrigue by an evil villain known as Genocide. Genocide is an interdimensional, parallel being. He is also a "spirit collector." In my series, he, and others like him, collect the spirits or souls of others.

Genocide bargains with Dark Storm for his spirit and tricks him with big words and smooth lies. Dark Storm and his spirit are stolen by Genocide. John Big Bear, Dark Storm's brother, is a wise medicine man, and when he learns of Dark Storm's kidnapping, he leaves this dimension and his earthly body to find his stolen brother.

To Big Bear's horror, when he does find Dark Storm he is doing Genocide's dirty work—he is Genocide's spiritual slave. To make a long story short, Big Bear breaks his brother free, rescues him, and brings him back to this dimension.

Dark Storm and Big Bear are now the Defenders of the Realm—a place that has had much of its spirit stolen, a place with little life.

TOUGHING IT OUT

Stephen Patrick Defazio, age 11

Hobbies: Collecting sports cards, playing guitar, sports, and video games **Favorite class:** math **Pet peeve:** tattletales **Favorite author:** Stephen King **Hero:** Eric Lindros of the Philadelphia Flyers **Dream:** To play professional football in the NFL

A few years ago I battled a terrifying illness and wasn't sure if I was even going to make it. I decided to write my story of toughing it out because even though it was the worst time in my life, I did get through it. I beat it! I'm still here and life is really good again. I hope that if you are going through a tough time, my story will help give you courage. If I can do it, so can you. So, never give up!

My "Tough" Situation

I was a pretty normal second-grader. I played soccer and did well in school. But in March I started getting these weird headaches—horrible headaches! They would start out by making me dizzy and sick to my stomach, then I would hear a terrible ringing in my ears and all light hurt my eyes. The headaches and dizziness were so bad that I had to quit baseball. After a few months of the headaches, I got this mysterious pain behind my right eye that hurt so bad it made me cry. By this time I was pretty scared. What was wrong with me?

My mom also got worried and took me to the doctor, who said that I just had "classic migraine headaches." My dad wasn't happy with this diagnosis, so he called his cousin, who is a doctor. Dr. Jim decided I should take a test called an MRI (this test helps the doctors see what's going on inside your head), which they scheduled for June 16, the first day of summer vacation—just my luck!

The last weeks of school were a total nightmare! I had headaches every day and I missed nine out of the last ten days of school. At our Field Day I collapsed and was taken to the nurse's office in a wheelchair. Everyone was staring and pointing and I was totally embarrassed and confused. Why was this happening to me?

Finally, June 16 came around and I went in for the MRI. I had to lay on a sliding table that moved inside a big machine that looked like a narrow tunnel and made lots of strange banging noises. Laying on that table, scared and wondering what was wrong with me, I felt like the test and the banging would never end. It seemed like forever, but it only took an hour.

When the results came back, we learned the scary news—there was a tumor growing behind my right eye. The tumor was already 1.5 centimeters in diameter—about the size of a dime! And that wasn't the worst news . . . the tumor might have cancer and would keep growing unless I had it taken out. I could tell the news was pretty bad because my mom was trying hard not to cry and my dad was very nervous. The doctors scheduled surgery for July 20, more than a month away!

Would They Turn Me into Frankenstein?

Everyone started treating me funny then. People constantly came over to visit and called on the phone. My mom got really upset whenever I got a headache, but the pain just kept getting worse every day. As my surgery date approached, I became even more nervous and scared than before.

I tried hard to act brave and not to show how scared I was. But when I was alone in my room I lay awake wondering what the doctors would to do to me in surgery. Would I look different? Would they mess up my eye? Would I end up looking like Frankenstein?

For the surgery, I had to go stay in a hospital in another town. It was almost impossible not to cry when I said good-bye to my sisters, and the ride to the hospital seemed so long. I'll never forget the night before the surgery—my mom and dad took me miniature golfing and mom kept hugging and kissing me. I could tell that she was really worried. Back in the hotel, people called like crazy, all sending me their love. That night I wished more than anything that I could be home in my own bed. Maybe it was all just a terrible nightmare and I would wake up in my bedroom and everything would be like before.

I fell asleep and the next thing I knew it was morning—time to go to the hospital. It was still dark outside and the hospital seemed huge and scary. At the start of the surgery the nurse put an I.V. (a needle and tube that puts medicine in your body) in my arm. That hurt a lot. Again, I tried hard not to cry because I didn't want to upset my mom even more. The nurse explained what was going to happen to me and asked if I had any questions. I was so nervous, and when I'm nervous I make jokes. So I said, "Is the surgery going to mess up my hair?" The doctors and nurses all laughed. Even my mom and dad smiled. Then they had to leave and I was alone.

The nurse put a mask on my face and told me to count. That's all I remember until I woke up with a terrible pain in my head. I didn't have a mirror, so I used my hands to try and figure out what had happened to me. I panicked as I felt the bandages completely covering my right eye. What did they do to me? What did I look like? Was my eye okay? The pain was really bad and I was crying hard, so the doctor gave me painkillers. The rest of the day was like a dream. I kept falling asleep and waking up and I never knew what time or even what day it was.

I Even Missed My Sisters! Unbelievable!

My mom stayed with me day and night. I was in a special care unit and the nurses checked on me all the time. They even brought me a Nintendo on wheels, but I was in so much pain I couldn't play at all. The doctors told my parents the good news and the bad news. The bad news was they couldn't remove the entire tumor, so they would have to keep checking it until I was eighteen or nineteen years old. The tumor had also eaten away some of my skull bone and exposed part of my brain. The good news was that the tumor didn't have any cancer and I could go home soon. I was excited about that. I really missed home . . . I even missed my sisters by then. I never thought that would happen!

When I got home there was a ton of people there to greet me. For weeks I had visitors every day, each with get-well presents for me. It was pretty cool, but I couldn't do anything but rest and let my surgery heal. Soon I was bored and tired of staying in the house. It was summer and I wanted to swim, ride my bike, and play outside with my friends, but I wasn't allowed to. I couldn't wait to go back to school and be with my friends again.

My "Normal" Life Goes Out the Window—Again!

Third grade started out pretty good, but then the headaches started again. I missed a lot of school and had to have more tests. No one could figure out why the headaches were back, so I had to see a headache specialist and try all kinds of medicines until the pain went away again.

My fourth-grade year also started out fine until my doctor tried a new headache medicine on me. The first day I took it, I came home from school and passed out. When I came to, it got harder and harder to breathe. My parents rushed me to the hospital where we found out that I had a severe allergic reaction to the medicine. By the next morning my allergic reaction had turned into full-blown pneumonia.

Over the next six months I got pneumonia four more times, I became allergic to all kinds of medicines, and I even developed asthma (a disease that makes it more difficult to breathe). I had to go to an allergy specialist and an asthma specialist and I had to breathe into a machine four times a day, use inhalers, and take all kinds of pills. I kept missing more school.

Being sick all the time made me really sad, scared, and even mad. My friends stopped coming over to play because they knew I was always sick. My mom tried to cheer me up saying, "You'll get through this. You're just having all your health problems now, so you won't have to have any when you're older. You're gonna live to be at least a hundred, just wait and see!" Somehow my mom did manage to make me feel better, and my sisters stayed with me and kept me company, but I was still very unhappy.

Just Let Me Be "Normal" Again

That time of my life was awful. I hated always being sick. I hated being rushed to the doctor's office because I couldn't breathe. Most of all, I hated coming back to school and having my friends act like I was a visitor in my own class. They would yell, "Hey, Stevie's here!" I was tired of being different. I didn't want to be the sick one anymore. I didn't want teachers always asking me if I was all right. I didn't want to go home every-day for lunch so I could take all my medicines and do my breathing treatments.

I wanted to be normal—just a plain, ordinary kid. I wanted to play football and other rough sports with the guys again. I wondered if my life would ever be like it was before. Every time I turned around there were new doctors, different tests, and lots of medicines. I was also pretty worried that I would be in the fourth grade forever. I had missed so many days at school. How would I ever catch up? I was miserable and scared. Would I be sick for the rest of my life?

My Big Comeback

That summer things started to turn around. I had a great tutor and I worked really hard. My mom was always giving me workbooks to do, which I complained about, but by the end of the summer I was caught up. It was hard to believe, but I was ready for the fifth grade! I felt happy and confident. I felt like I used to feel before the tumor.

I'm now in the fifth grade and so far it's been a great year. Somehow things got straightened out in me. I still have allergies, but they don't bother me that much. My asthma is completely under control and my headaches are much better. I go for my next tumor tests in June, but for now I'm not going to worry about it.

Somehow, some way, I got through this. Lots of people helped me and gave me love. Often you don't realize how much your family really loves you until something bad happens. I didn't give up either. Sometimes things may seem really, really bad, but if you just hang in there, you'll get through it. Believe me, I know. I got through some pretty bad stuff and now I'm happy to say that I'm just your plain, ordinary, normal fifth-grader.

I'm a New Man

But in many ways I am very different from "normal" fifth-graders. My experience taught me a lot:

★ I don't get upset anymore when little things don't go my way. If the video store doesn't have the game I want, that's okay, I can get it some other time.

★ I don't complain much anymore. When I was at the hospital I saw so many little kids, two and three years old, bald, with tubes coming out of them. No matter how bad I thought I had it, many had it even worse. That's the sad thing I learned: There are a lot of kids out there who have much bigger problems than I had.

★ I know that I want to help sick kids someday—to give them hope, to make them laugh, and to help them not be so afraid.

Life is better now. No one makes a big fuss when I walk into my classroom anymore. It's terrific not to have my mom and the teachers always watching me with worried looks on their faces and asking me if I'm feeling all right. And, the most amazing thing of all has happened. My mom just signed me up to play football! I couldn't be happier.

FEED YOUR FACE
CRAZY KITCHEN CONCOCTIONS

Martin Erlic, age 7

✂ **Hobbies:** playing computer games, drawing, skiing, soccer, reading, acting in school plays, and writing books ✎ **Favorite class:** math and art ✏ **Favorite author:** Chris Van Allsburg ☹ **Pet peeve:** I don't like eating spiders (just kidding) ♫ **Hero:** Hercules and my daddy ❁ **Dream:** to open a "Muffin Surprise" in Croatia, to learn about physics, astronomy, electronics, and engineering, and to write a cookbook for boys

Believe it or not, guys can have fun in the kitchen! Some guys don't like to cook—maybe because they think it's too hard. But it's not—it's easy and totally fun! With my cool recipes and by doing your own crazy experiments in the kitchen, you'll never be bored again (or hungry either)! You can make weird things like "applizza"—that's just pizza with apples and cheese for toppings. Just use your imagination to make and do fun things in the kitchen—and then eat them.

I first got interested in cooking because my mom has her own cooking show on TV and gets to make up her own recipes. She showed me how fun and easy it is to make up my own recipes too. Now I do it all the time. My mom likes to cook because she can do it with her friends or family and then eat up all her work! My dad likes to cook because he likes trying different, unusual things, like ostrich steaks. My uncle says it's more fun to cook when you wear a chef's hat.

I like to cook because I can make exactly what I feel like eating, not what someone else wants to make for me. Plus I get to use my creativity and have some fun. I even share my concoctions with my friends—and now I'm sharing them with you!

How to Have Fun in Your Kitchen

There are a lot of things I like about the kitchen—the bright lights, the yummy smells, the warm oven. But my favorite thing is the refrigerator because there's so much good food in it. Cooking in the kitchen is a great way to spend time with my family. We get to hang out together, talk, and have fun. Here are a few of the other ways I have fun in the kitchen:

✿ When I crack eggs, I crack them the wrong way so they splatter on me. You usually get a little messy when you cook—that's part of the fun.

✿ When you're working with flour, sometimes it overflows onto the counter. It looks like snow and you can draw in it with your finger. I draw happy faces, dogs, babies, and even dinosaurs.

✿ You can mix baking soda with vinegar to make a bubbling lava mixture. All you have to do is put a few spoonfuls of baking soda in a bowl and add water.

✿ It's also fun to add exotic flavors to muffins and pancakes you're making. The flavors I like the best come from adding blueberries, mangos, carrots, melon, apples, orange peels, lemon peels, and lime peels. Use your imagination—think of the lemon as the sun, the orange as a basketball, the carrot as a snake, the melon as Humpty Dumpty, and the mango as a squishy, gooey egg yolk!

All you have to do is mix your favorite things with food—it's that easy, dude!

Kitchen Survival Skills

Cooking is fun to do, but remember the safety rules:

♨ Watch out for hot things so you don't get burned.

- Be careful using knives. Your parents should use the knives for you, or at least watch you while you learn to use them.
- An adult should always be with you in the kitchen.

Creating Your Own Crazy Kitchen Concoctions!

Recipes are easy to make up yourself. Think of your favorite things like playing on the computer, reading, math, watching TV, soccer, hockey, skiing, or skating. Use your interests to come up with recipe ideas!

If you like soccer, you can make a soccer ball pancake. If you like math, you can make a calculator sandwich, using salami to make the numbers (just don't put a real calculator in the sandwich). If you like hockey, you can make a Jell-O hockey puck. If you like skiing, you can make chocolate skis from French fries dipped in chocolate.

MARTIN'S MAGNIFICENT MUNCHIES

PIZZA FACE

This is a good recipe for parties, lunches, and snacks.

1 bread slice

2 tablespoons ketchup or spaghetti sauce

1 cheese slice, white cheddar

3 cheese squares, orange cheddar

5 sweet red pepper slices

1 leaf of lettuce

butter knife

Method: Using a butter knife, put ketchup on the bread. Cut up the cheese slice and use it for the mouth. Place cheese squares in position for the eyes and nose. Place the red pepper slices on top for the hair. Place lettuce under the nose for a mustache. Serves 1.

PB&J DINOSAUR

You can make different kinds of dinosaurs like Tyrannosaurus Rex, Brontosaurus, Stegosaurus, Pterosaur, or Velociraptor.

2 bread slices

1 tablespoon peanut butter

1 tablespoon jam

butter knife

Method: Using a butter knife, put peanut butter and jam on the two slices of bread. Then cut the bread into the shape of your favorite dinosaur. Makes 1 dinosaur.

GOLF BALL SANDWICH

You can take this golfing and eat while you play!

2 bread slices

1/4 cup peanut butter

10 mini chocolate chips

butter knife

Method: Place two slices of bread on a plate and make a peanut butter sandwich. Cut a golf ball shape from the sandwich. Eat the crust so you don't waste it. Sprinkle mini chocolate chips on the ball. Serves 1.

TOWER OF PEANUT BUTTER

I like this giant sandwich because there's tons of food to eat! If you're really hungry eat this sandwich or else!

10 bread slices

10 tablespoons peanut butter

10 tablespoons jam

1 grape

butter knife

1 toothpick

Method: Place the bread slices side by side. Using a butter knife, spread peanut butter and jam on the slices. Pile bread slices on top of each other.

Put a toothpick through the grape and stick the toothpick through the top of the sandwich. Serves 4.

STUFFED SALAMI ROLL

My dad showed me how to make this recipe—one of his favorites.

    1 slice salami

    1 stick of cheese (cut to the size of your finger)

    1 teaspoon mayonnaise

    butter knife

    1 toothpick

Method: Using a butter knife, put mayonnaise on the salami, then add the cheese stick. Roll it up, and put a toothpick through it to hold it together. Serves 1.

FRUIT SOY SHAKE

If you're thirsty, drink this or else!

    1 cup soy milk

    (Soy milk is like regular milk, but made from soybeans. You can buy it in most grocery stores in the regular milk section, or in the health food section.)

    5 slices apple

    5 slices orange

    1 whole banana

    blender

Method: Put soy milk in the blender. Put apple, orange, and banana in the blender. Blend until smooth. Serves 1.

PIZZA TARTS

These tarts are yummy and delicious. Eat it! And I mean it, eat!

    5 tart shells, baked (follow directions on the box)

    5 teaspoons ketchup or spaghetti sauce

    1 cup shredded cheese

    1/2 cup pepperoni, sliced

butter knife

Method: Using a butter knife, spread ketchup inside the tart shells. Sprinkle cheese and pepperoni in tart shells. Bake at 300°F for 5 minutes. Serves 5.

SOCCER BALLCAKES

Get a soccer ball, put pancakes on it, then eat it! Just kidding!

    1 pancake

    (Most pancake mixes have the recipe right on the bag. You may need your parents' help the first time you make one.)

    1/4 cup chocolate syrup

Method: Put the pancake on a plate. Place circles of chocolate in different sections of the pancake, until it looks like a soccer ball. Serves 1.

CRISPY "FIRE" SQUARES

These squares are hot and spicy, so beware! Your mouth will burn! You must get water quickly!

    1/4 cup butter

    1/8 cup honey

    5 cups marshmallows

    pinch of cayenne

    7 cups rice cereal (like Rice Krispies)

    medium-size pot

    casserole pan

    butter knife

Method: On medium heat on your stove, melt the butter, honey, and marshmallows in your pot. Add the cayenne. Stir well. Add the rice cereal. Put the mixture into your casserole pan. Put warm water on your hands and press the mixture down until flat and smooth. Let it cool. Then, using a butter knife, cut into squares. Serves 10.

BOWLING BALL TOAST

Wait until the toast cools down before you use it. Don't touch the hot toast. Ouch! Let your parents help you.

> 1 piece of burnt toast
> coffee mug
> butter knife

Method: Have parents burn toast in toaster. Use a mug to punch out a circle from the toast. Using a butter knife, cut three holes in the toast, for finger holes. Serves 1.

JELL-O PUCK

If you put this hockey puck on ice and whip it with a hockey stick, it will splatter and not taste so good.

> 1 small package purple Jell-O
> butter knife

Method: Follow the directions on the Jell-O box. When it's done, use a butter knife to cut 4 big circles out of the Jell-O. Makes 4 hockey pucks. Serves 4.

TENNIS RACKET BREAKFAST

Don't use this for tennis—it will fall apart. (JOKE: What did the tennis ball say to the tennis racket? Answer: "Stop making all that racket!")

> 1 large pancake
> 12 strings of black licorice
> 1 piece of toast
> butter knife

Method: Put pancake on a plate. Lay 6 licorice strings across the pancake, then place the other 6 licorice strings across the pancake in the other direction, so the strings cross. Using a butter knife, cut the toast in half and place it touching the pancake's edge to make a handle. Serves 1.

BASKETBAFFLE

I like maple syrup on this basketball. (Joke: What did the basketball hoop say to the basketball? Answer: "Nice of you to drop in.")

1 round waffle

2 black licorice strings

Method: Put the waffle on the plate. Put licorice strings on the waffle and curve them into basketball stripes. Serves 1.

SWEET SWIMMING POOL

Feel like diving into a sweet swimming pool? (Joke: What did the diving board say to the swimming pool? Answer: "I'm having a splash.")

1 large package blue Jell-O

10 Smarties or M&Ms

Method: Follow the directions on the Jell-O package. Pour finished Jell-O in a glass bowl. Sprinkle Smarties or M&Ms over the top of the Jell-O. Serves 5.

CUCUMBER CAR

Warning: *Take the toothpicks out before you eat the car! And don't use this for a real race, since it would get squished by the other cars!*

1/2 cucumber

4 round banana slices

1 round carrot slice

1 M&M

pinch of alfalfa sprouts

Method: Place cucumber on a plate. Stick toothpicks into the middle of banana slices to make wheels. Stick the banana wheels to the cucumber. Place the carrot slice on top of the cucumber for the seat. Put the M&M right in front of the seat for the steering wheel. Put the alfalfa sprouts on the back of the cucumber for the exhaust. Serves 2.

BITE THE BARK DUST

This is a good-for-you snack.

1/2 cup Life cereal

1/4 cup chocolate syrup

Method: Put Life cereal in a bowl. Cover the cereal with chocolate syrup. Stir well until coated. Refrigerate until the chocolate gets hard. Serves 1.

KETCHUP RICE CASSEROLE

When I took this Ketchup Rice Casserole over to my grandparents' house, they loved it.

1 tablespoon oil

3 cups cooked rice

1 1/2 cups ketchup

3 cups mozzarella

small casserole pan

Method: Spread the oil in the casserole pan. Put 1 cup rice in the pan. Then layer 1/2 cup ketchup and 1 cup mozzarella. Layer ingredients two more times. Bake at 400°F for 7 minutes. Serves 7.

These are all easy, fun, tasty recipes that any guy could make for himself—perfect for after-school snacks, or you could even surprise your parents by making one for dinner. Wouldn't that shock them? So, time to get cooking!

SURVIVING SISTERS

Michael J. Adinolfi Jr., age 12

Hobbies: baseball, soccer, basketball, football, Tae Kwon Do, sleepovers, playing with friends, street hockey, computers **Favorite class:** geography **Favorite books:** *The Witches* and *Hatchet* **Hero:** my dad **Dream:** to become a professional hockey player

Do you have sisters? Are you baffled by their behavior? Do you pull your hair out trying to live with them? Sisters can be predictable or unpredictable—your cruelest tormentor or your strongest ally. I have three sisters, so I know how it feels. Over the years I've figured out how to survive living with them—how to get my way, how to get revenge, and most of all, how to get along.

Whether you have been living with sisters for years or are about to have a brand-new sister in your life, this chapter is for you. Sometimes it's hard being a boy in a house of girls, but my expert advice should help get you through it.

Having Sisters Is a Drag When . . .

. . . they gang up to tease you and hurt your feelings.

. . . they butt into your private life.

. . . they sneak in your room and mess it up.

. . . they borrow things without asking—just to annoy you.

. . . you fight with them and you get hurt.

. . . they bug you constantly to play boring games with them.

. . . they want to play with you and your friends, but you want privacy.

. . . they get angry at you.

. . . they don't accept you as you are.

. . . they ignore you and you have no say at all.

My sisters take life way too seriously. They should have more fun. Instead of having fun they worry about their hair and clothes. They have a million pairs of shoes in their closet. I only have one pair of sneakers and one pair of dress shoes (that I hate wearing). And they still go crazy trying to find something to wear. If I was allowed to wear sneakers and jeans 365 days a year, I would be a very happy guy.

Tips to Stop Them from . . .

. . . Teasing You in Front of Your Friends

Do you have sisters who bug you when you have friends over? My sisters do. They love to embarrass me in front of my friends. They will mention a girl's name, saying that I like her, trying to embarrass me. This kind of behavior makes my face get red from anger. I think they do it because they want attention and want to play with me and my friends. If this happens to you, just ignore them, or if you want, include them in whatever you're doing. This should stop them from embarrassing you.

. . . Blabbing Your Secrets

Do your sisters blab your secrets? Here's some advice to keep them from going out in the open. First of all, you don't have to tell anyone your secrets. But if they do know some of your secrets, you could bring up one of their embarrassing experiences. Then their plan probably will backfire and blow up in their faces. If that doesn't work, give them some money so they won't tell anyone.

. . . Messing with Your Stuff

Some sisters love getting into your journal and scribbling in it. They might even mess up your collection of baseball cards. Some sisters just don't understand about a boy's privacy, so explaining the meaning of the words "keep out" on your bedroom door is very important. I think the most logical solution to this problem is to be respectful of your sisters' belongings and be clear with them that they should respect yours. If they don't respect your stuff, then when you tell your parents, your sisters won't have any excuses for their behavior (e.g., "But he does it to me, too").

Having Sisters Is Great When . . .
. . . you know they really love you.
. . . they comfort you when you get hurt.
. . . they help with your homework (older sisters).
. . . they take care of you when you're sick.
. . . you help your younger sisters succeed and they look up to you.
. . . you show support for your older sisters.
. . . they help prepare you for what is ahead of you in life.
. . . you help them through their frustrations in life.
. . . you realize that it's better than not having brothers or sisters.
. . . you have someone to play with.

I like having sisters because when I'm lonely I always play with one of them. We have fun playing games like Monopoly or Scrabble. My sisters also take my side in fights.

The greatest thing about sisters is you can always count on them. I play street hockey with my sister Kristen. She is the only girl who plays, and I have to admit she does play like one of us guys. One time I got hurt playing hockey and she was the first one there to help me. When she sprinted into the house for a bag of ice, I knew that she really cares about me.

Another time my sisters came to the rescue was when a baby-sitter was taking care of us and teaching us a game on our trampoline called "Crack the Egg." We let too many people on the trampoline together and I hurt my neck. I wasn't hurt very badly, but the baby-sitter really freaked out and was going to call 911. Even though my sister knew we were all going to get into big trouble with our parents because of me, she stayed calm and helped me into the house. She didn't get mad at me at all but just calmed down the baby-sitter and convinced her that I would be okay (which I was). That experience showed me again that my sisters will stick by me through thick and thin.

Getting Revenge Versus Getting Along

Anyone who has a sister knows that every once in a while they drive you absolutely crazy. You have two choices when this happens: You can either get them back or you can get along.

Getting Revenge

This option may feel good when you do it, but it will most likely get you in trouble or cause your sister to get revenge on you. So think long and hard before you go down this road.

Property Violations

There are lots of revenge tactics I've tried in the past. I've snuck into my sisters' rooms and dumped their perfume down the sink. I've hidden their dolls. I've messed up their Barbies' hairdos and I've even painted their Barbies' heads. I've stolen their candy and eaten it all. I sometimes repeat everything they say—that really annoys them.

Sleepover Scares

Do your sisters have sleepovers at your house? Well mine do, and some of their friends are nice and some are whiny brats. I like to annoy the whiny ones. Late at night I sneak into my sister's room and scare the daylights out of her and her friends.

Don't Get Physical

When getting revenge on your sister, don't ever react by hitting her because that's a freeway ticket to your room and getting grounded. This is not a news flash! If you made the decision to hit or push your sister, you might as well just head for your room. It might be a long time before you see daylight again.

TALES OF REVENGE

Painting their doll's head came to me while sitting in the car at the gas station. I saw these two teenagers with messed up, out-of-this-world purple and pink hairdos. I started laughing myself sick and couldn't wait to get my paint set out in case my sisters started giving me trouble.

One Halloween I went to the freezer and snuck a few pieces of my sister's candy. Every day I took a few more pieces, little by little. By Thanksgiving all her candy was gone, but she had no idea who the candy thief was. There was no evidence left!

Getting Along

Listen

Getting along with sisters can be pretty tough, but it's better for everyone in the long run. To get along with her, try listening to her side of the argument. Instead of fighting with her, try agreeing with what she says. You'll be amazed at how much better this works than fighting.

Respect Her Privacy

When your sister has a sleepover, show her some respect by leaving her and her friends alone while they polish their nails and smell up the room with their stinky perfume. It always amazes me that they waste time doing that stuff when they could be having real fun, like playing hockey and baseball. But if you want them to leave you alone while you hang out with your friends, you should leave them alone with theirs.

Play Together

Try playing together sometimes. If you have video games, play a game that allows two players; it won't kill you. If it doesn't allow two players, then take turns playing the video game. Listen to your parents and try sharing some of your toys. If you share your toys, they'll probably share theirs too. We have the most fun playing with my Legos. My dad even built a huge Legos table in our basement where our whole family can sit and build together.

Catch a Good Mood

Sisters can often get themselves into bad moods—so if you want to borrow something, ask for their help, or play with them, try catching them when they are in a good mood.

On Your Side

If you can manage to get along with your sister, then when you have trouble with kids from school or with your parents, she'll help you and be on your side. It's always good to have an ally.

How Can I Protect My Privacy?

First, be sure you're respecting your sisters' privacy, if you want them to respect yours. If you do respect their privacy and have tried asking them to respect yours, but it hasn't worked, you may have to turn to your parents for help. Recently, I asked my parents to buy me a new lock for my door. They did, and now this lock keeps my sisters from barging right in whenever they feel like it. Another good trick I use is shoe boxes! I keep all my really important, private things in shoe boxes that I stack in the back of my closet. For some reason, my sisters never seem to look in the shoe boxes. Maybe they think they're just shoes, or maybe it's too much trouble. You could even tape them closed if you're really worried.

How Can I Stop Them from Picking on Me?

You could insult them in a way that will make them not want to talk to you anymore. You could tell on them. But the best method is to ignore them.

How Can I Get Them to Share with Me?

Asking politely sometimes gets them to share things. If you share your stuff with them when they ask, they will probably let you use their stuff when you ask. You might have to remind them of what you shared with them. This method always works for me and I think you'll have good luck with it.

How Can I Get Them to Leave Me Alone?

Say that you're busy and that you need to concentrate. Ask if they will leave the room. If that doesn't work, say you will play with them later. When they leave the room, get back to work. If that still doesn't work, you may need to find your own private spot—a treehouse, a secret fort in the basement or backyard, under the stairs—anywhere that you can escape them and be alone. You might start looking for your secret alone spot now so you know where to go later when it's an emergency.

How Can I Get Them to Do Stuff with Me When I'm Bored?

The most obvious way is to ask them if you can play with them. However, you might have to play whatever they want to play. If what they're playing is a dumb or boring game, just quit.

Don't bother asking them to play what you want. You're probably not so desperate that you need to do something that you don't even like. Or, if you think you can convince them, ask if you could take turns. You could say, "If we play your game first, then we should play my game next." This might work.

How Can I Stop Them from Bossing Me Around?

You can ignore them and block out what they say. Act like you can't hear them—that really gets them steamed. Usually they won't even talk to you after the the silent treatment, so you can say "bye-bye" to them bossing you around.

How Can I Get Some Alone Time with My Parents?

The best policy is to just be honest with your parents. Without being whiny or angry, tell them that you feel like you're being ignored and ask if you can spend some real quality time alone with them. This usually works for me. My parents usually find the time to spend alone with me after I tell them how I feel.

Conclusion

There are some very unenjoyable and unfair times living with three sisters, but I don't know what my life would be like if they weren't a part of it. I do miss them when they are gone for a long time, so that must mean I really care about them. I know they care about me. So, even though sisters can be a pain, I think they're actually worth the trouble. If you learn how to make peace with them, you will have loyal friends for life.

PHILOGRAPHY
GETTING YOUR HERO'S AUTOGRAPH

Timothy Eng, age 14

✀ **Hobbies:** writing, surfing the Internet, bicycling, basketball, collecting autographs, watching movies

📖 **Favorite book:** *The Autobiography of Malcolm X*

☹ **Pet peeve:** when people act phoney and pretend to be someone they are not   ✍ **Hero:** Jeff Ota, a research engineer at NASA Ames Research Center and the youngest and only Asian-American on the East San Jose school board

❀ **Dream:** to be a teacher so I can make a difference in the world

Boys of America, are you looking for a really cool, unique hobby . . . one that can put you in touch with the likes of Michael Jordan, Tiger Woods, and David Letterman? What is this mysterious activity called? Well, actually, philography!

Yes, you read correctly. No, you don't have to pronounce it in order to do it. Philography means the love of writing. In everyday language, it also means "autograph collecting."

How I Got Started

I first started collecting autographs when I was eight years old. My parents decided that they wanted me to practice cursive writing during the summer. So instead of copying sentences from a book, I decided that I would rather write letters to famous celebrities, hoping that they would write back and send me their autographs.

Collecting autographs is not just a cool and fun hobby, it also has other benefits (which especially impress adults). For instance, you will learn about a lot of great people, and it gives you a chance to practice writing. Another great thing is that it's cheap—all you need is paper, a pen, envelopes, and stamps—so you can save your cash for other things.

Getting Yourself Started

First you have to decide who you want to write to. This is really fun. Remember, the possibilities are endless! Over the years, I have written letters to famous authors like Tomie dePaola, Shel Silverstein, and Jack Prelutsky, Nobel Prize-winners like Dr. Linus Pauling, university presidents like Dr. Chang-Lin Tien of the University of California at Berkeley, and famous professional athletes like David Robinson of the San Antonio Spurs. I have written to astronauts, television news anchors and reporters, and countless others.

Top Ten Best Groups to Write to

1. Hollywood celebrities: actors and actresses, producers, directors, comedians, and other TV entertainers (for example, game show hosts and even voices of cartoon characters).
2. Athletes: famous athletes in football, basketball, baseball, hockey, boxing, soccer, and just about any other sport you can think of. And don't forget the Olympic champions!
3. Politicians: U.S. presidents and first ladies, senators and other Congress members, governors, mayors, and foreign heads of state.
4. Professionals: scientists, architects, astronauts, and Nobel Prize-winners, TV news anchors and reporters.
5. Religious leaders: whoever inspires you.
6. Fashion designers: your favorites like Tommy Hilfiger, Ralph Lauren, Pierre Cardin, etc.
7. Authors: of children's books or adult books.

8. Music professionals: musicians, composers, and even rock stars. Don't forget to consider stars from all kinds of music styles.

9. Kings and queens: from around the world.

10. If you are a member of an ethnic minority, you might be interested in collecting letters from famous individuals of a particular ethnic background.

What Do I Write in My Letter?

When you write your letter, you want to let the famous person know that you know something about him or her, so be sure to read a book or magazine article about the person. In the letter, ask them questions about what you always wanted to know about them. When you know something about the person to whom you are writing, you will find it easier to think of questions to ask. Try to be original and think of a question that no one has ever asked before. If you make your letter interesting, your chances of getting a reply will be much better.

My Top Ten Favorite Questions to Ask

1. What was your favorite subject in school when you were my age? (Be sure to mention how old you are in your letters.)
2. Did you like to do homework?
3. How much allowance did you get at my age?
4. Do you ever see any of your childhood friends?
5. What's the most important advice your parents gave you?
6. How did you spend your summers when you were my age?
7. What was the best birthday present you ever got?
8. What other kinds of work have you considered doing?
9. When you were my age, what did you want to be when you grew up?
10. Is there something you still want to do in your life?

When you write your letters, be sure to tell the celebrity a bit about yourself, like how old you are, what grade you're in, where you go to school, what your favorite subjects are, etc. Be sure to include your name and address (especially on all materials that you include with your letters) because sometimes things get separated.

Keep your letters relatively short and to the point. Celebrities are usually extremely busy people, and long letters tend to be set aside to read "tomorrow." Never send food to celebrities. After all, would you eat chocolate chip cookies given to you by a total stranger?

Last, be sure to make a photocopy of your letter before sending it, so you can remember what you said in your letter. Photocopies of letters you sent look great next to the response you eventually receive from the celebrity.

Where Do I Find Celebrity Addresses?

This part might seem really hard, but actually you can find the mailing addresses of celebrities in many places. Paperback books sold in bookstores have many addresses of celebrities. The most popular books that I have run across include the following:

1. *Children's Authors and Illustrators* by Barbara Allman and Marsha Elyn Jurca. Published by Frank Schaffer.
2. *The Address Book: How to Reach Anyone Who Is Anyone* by Michael Levine. Published by Perigee Books.
3. *The Celebrity Phone Book* by Scott and Barbara Siegel. Published by Penguin Books.

The *Who's Who* directories are a great resource that you can find at your local public library. These directories contain brief biographies and mailing addresses of thousands of famous people in tons of different areas. The information is updated every few years.

Also at your local public library, you may be able to find the following helpful magazines: *Biography Today* (a monthly magazine), *Current Biography Magazine* (monthly), and *Current Biography Yearbook* (annual).

How Do I Take Care of
My Valuable Autograph Collection?

Okay, so now you have your letter from Charles Barkley, and you want to take care of it. If you want to make sure that your autograph collection maintains a high value, then you need to do the following:

1. Place letters in a clear plastic enclosure to protect them from sunlight.
2. Do not cut, staple, glue, or tape any letters or autographed photographs that you receive from a famous personality.
3. Do not cut signatures out of a letter or document.   ·
4. Never use paper clips or rubberbands on autographed documents, because both will leave stains.
5. Never leave autographed material in direct sunlight, even if documents are framed in glass. Sun will discolor the paper.
6. Never use plastic sprays, varnish, or shellac to cover and preserve any autographed document.

Are the Autographs Really Worth a Lot of Money?

The answer is yes—they really can be worth a lot, especially after the person isn't alive anymore. However, the greatest thing about autograph collecting comes not from financial gain but from holding history in your hand. A piece of paper that Tom Hanks, Robin Williams, Bill Clinton, Michael Jordan, or Brett Favre touched definitely has a certain magic.

Will My Heroes Really Write Back?

The greatest thing about philography is getting a response. In the dozens of letters that I have written over the years, I have always received a response from celebrities. Occasionally the letters, cards, and photos that are sent to me will take several weeks or even months to arrive. A basketball card that I sent to David Robinson for his autograph took six months before I got it back. But it did come eventually—you just need to be patient.

Occasionally, letters you write might even change your life! In 1982 Samantha Smith, a ten-year-old American schoolgirl, wrote from her home in Manchester, Maine, to Soviet leader Yuri Andropov. In her letter Samantha said that she was worried that the U.S. and the U.S.S.R. would fight a nuclear war. In a very touching letter, Samantha asked Andropov, "Why do you want to conquer the whole world, or at least our country?"

Andropov responded to Samantha in a very diplomatic letter in which he claimed that his country's intentions were peaceful. Andropov invited Samantha to come and visit his country to see life in the Soviet Union on a firsthand basis. Can you imagine Samantha's reaction? She met top Kremlin officials, had lunch with the first woman cosmonaut, and saw the Kirov Ballet in Leningrad. Samantha was a natural ambassador.

The visit was also a triumph for Andropov and the Soviet Union, for it brought the letter and Andropov's skillful response into public view and generated a wave of goodwill toward the Soviet Union. When Samantha appeared on prime-time talk shows in the U.S., her honesty helped to strengthen relations between the U.S. and the Soviet Union.

So you never know what can happen when you send a letter to a celebrity! You might receive a pair of athletic sneakers from a professional basketball player or you may be like Samantha Smith and receive an invitation to visit a foreign country as the guest of a head of state! So keep on writing, and have fun.

A GENTLEMAN'S GUIDE TO LIFE

Teddis Bailey, age 11

✂ **Hobbies:** drawing, basketball, football, and playing with my dog Jake ✎ **Favorite class:** English 📖 **Favorite book:** *Young Martin Luther King, Jr.* ☹ **Pet peeve:** when people talk improperly on national television ♜ **Hero:** my mother and God ❁ **Dream:** to play professional football

Jerehemy Diggs, age 11

✂ **Hobbies:** swimming and riding bikes ✎ **Favorite class:** English and science ✏ **Favorite author:** R. L. Stine ☹ **Pet peeve:** playing Sega ♜ **Hero:** Curt Henning ❁ **Dream:** to have all the money in the world

Erick Harris, age 12

✂ **Hobbies:** basketball, football, jumping rope, television, running laps, talking ✎ **Favorite class:** math and science ✏ **Favorite author:** R. L. Stine ☹ **Pet peeve:** kids doing drugs ♜ **Hero:** Superman ❁ **Dream:** to become a professional basketball player, and to have peace in the world

gentleman *n*. A polite, gracious, or considerate man with high standards of correct behavior.

To us, being a gentleman means being polite, respectful, and nice in public. We try our best to be gentlemen for everyone—our parents, our teachers, people we meet for the first time, and especially girls! We've discovered that being a gentleman earns you respect and privileges from adults. Want to borrow the car? Being a gentleman will really help. And acting like a gentleman is great for getting attention and admiration from girls. Just ask any girl you know . . . they all love a gentleman!

If you don't learn how to behave like a gentleman you could get yourself in embarrassing situations or miss great opportunities. If you don't know how to act when you are in public or out on a date, then you will probably embarrass yourself and whoever you are with. We know that the ladies don't want no mess, and if you like a girl, but don't know how to treat her, she will probably think you're just a plain fool. We hope our chapter shows other boys and men how to be gentlemen and why it will make their lives better!

Are You a Gentleman or a Jerk? Take Our Quiz!

Select your answers, then add up your points.

1. On your first date with a girl, you . . .

a) . . . show up smelling and looking your best. You have flowers for her and tell her she looks great.

b) . . . tell all your friends to meet you at a pizza place. When you go to get her, she's not ready yet. You tell her to hurry up because your friends are waiting.

c) . . . are running late after a game of basketball with your friends, so you skip the shower and race to her house. You're ten minutes late and smell pretty funky, but she won't care . . . girls love jocks, right?

2. You get on the bus and there's only one seat left. There's an elderly man struggling up the aisle toward the seat, his arms full of groceries. You're closer to the seat than he is, so you . . .

a) . . . race to the seat and take it. Too bad old guy!

b) . . . let the man have the seat and you stand.

c) . . . ask the man if you can help him, you give him the empty seat, and hold his groceries for him.

3. **You're watching TV when your mom comes home from work. The TV room is a mess and she looks tired, so you . . .**

a) . . . pick up your mess and then go outside to play.

b) . . . tell her to sit down and you make her some tea. While she's relaxing, you clean up the room and start working on dinner.

c) . . . ignore her and turn up the TV.

4. **Your teacher is very sick and is out of school for a week. Your class has a substitute teacher, so you . . .**

a) . . . encourage your class to do what the substitute asks and make a card to send to your sick teacher.

b) . . . make the substitute's life a total nightmare. Your whole class plays pranks on her, goofs off, and never does what she says. When your teacher returns, she has tons of work to catch up on and wishes she'd stayed home longer!

c) . . . behave yourself with the substitute and ignore your classmates, who are totally disruptive.

How Did You Do?

Add up your score:

1.	a)	3 points	b)	2 points	c)	1 point
2.	a)	1 point	b)	2 points	c)	3 points
3.	a)	2 points	b)	3 points	c)	1 point
4.	a)	3 points	b)	1 point	c)	2 points

What your score means:

4-6 Man, do you need some help! If you keep this up, you'll be grounded, suspended, and you'll never get a girlfriend. You better read on, my friend!

7-10 Not too bad. You're not a perfect gentleman, but you're not a total jerk either. A little work and you'll have it.

11-12 You are a true gentleman. You've got style, you've got class. Life is looking good for you. This chapter will just help you polish your skills!

Tips for Being a Gentleman on a Date

Being a gentleman to girls is great for you because girls will actually like you. If you like a girl, she'll probably notice you if you act like a gentleman. If you already have a girlfriend, using these tips will make it easier for you to keep her.

Tip 1: Always be on time.

Tip 2: Be nice. Actually, be on your very best behavior.

Tip 3: Always smell good and dress nicely. First impressions are very important . . . with her family too.

Tip 4: Tell her she looks great, smells great, etc.

Tip 5: If she's rushing, tell her to relax. You're not in a hurry.

Tip 6: Bring her a small but thoughtful present. Flowers picked from your house or a card are always good. (See "The Scoop on Girls" chapter for good gift ideas.)

Tip 7: Open doors and pull out chairs for her (some girls don't like this, so try it once and see if she's into it).

Tip 8: If you go to her house for dinner, help out. Set and clear the table, help cook, and always wash some dishes.

Tip 9: Be someone she can talk to. Don't laugh at her or make fun of her. Be someone she can trust.

Tip 10: Don't ever talk badly about her to your friends. That's rude and she'll never trust you again.

More Dating Tips

Q: Does a gentleman always pay when he takes a girl out?
A: Girls today might be offended if you pay for everything. Plus, you'll go bankrupt fast. It's best to "go dutch," which means you each pay for your own food and movie tickets.

Q: How does a gentleman tell a girl how fine she is?
A: A true gentleman gives girls compliments without making them uncomfortable. Say something respectful, like "You look nice today" or "That's a cool outfit."

Tips for Being a Gentleman with Your Parents

Being a gentleman for your parents is great for you because you won't get in trouble or get grounded so much. You'll also earn trust and privileges. Your parents will respect you more and treat you less like a little kid.

Tip 1: Do your chores and pick up after yourself without being asked.

Tip 2: Make your parents proud by making the honor roll and being a good student.

Tip 3: Hold open the door for them if their hands are full.

Tip 4: Offer to baby-sit your younger siblings and cousins if your parents need a break. Your parents might even pay you or give you special privileges.

Tip 5: Do nice things for them every once in a while. Run a hot bath for them after a long day. Surprise them by straightening up their room. For a good birthday present, clean the house!

Tip 6: Help work on the yard. Weeding, mowing, working in a vegetable garden will really impress your parents.

Tip 7: Don't fight with your brothers and sisters in front of your parents. It drives them crazy and you'll get in trouble.

Tip 8: Be polite to their friends and to other family members. This will make your parents very proud of you.

Tip 9: Always use good manners at the dinner table.

Tip 10: Give your parents the respect they deserve.

Tips for Being a Gentleman with Other Adults

Teachers—Do your best on your schoolwork, have a good attitude with the teacher, and try to help out in class whenever you can. Being a gentleman in class will help your grades.

Neighbors—A gentleman is respected and admired by his neighbors. To earn this respect, try to be helpful and friendly. For example, if a neighbor's grass is tall, you could ask, "Can I mow your lawn for you?" They'll probably even pay you, and the rest of the neighborhood will know what a great guy you are.

Coaches—Be on time to practices, don't miss games, and do your best to follow your coaches' advice and respect their decisions. Never fight or injure opponents on purpose. Being a gentleman will help you stay off the bench and in the game, and you'll have a lot more fun.

Strangers—It's important to be a gentleman when you see a person struggling. A gentleman always asks if someone needs help. You never know when you might need a stranger's help.

If you still have any doubts that being a gentleman will improve your life, give our tips a try. We're sure you'll find that being a gentleman will help you get everything you want out of life.

DAZED & CONFUSED

DRUGS AND US

Samuel Kirk, age 10

✂ **Hobbies:** reading, playing wall ball, trick-or-treating, writing, drawing, and playing Doom ✎ **Favorite class:** gym and social studies 📖 **Favorite book:** *The Body* ♫ **Hero:** Stan Lee and Mark Hamill because I love the movie *Star Wars* ✿ **Dream:** To be a best-selling writer

Drugs. Whether you've tried them or not, whether you think you might or know you never will, whether you know someone who does them or have never seen them at all, drugs are something we boys all have to face at some point. Everyone knows that using drugs is not a good idea. They're illegal and if you get caught with them you could be arrested. Even if you don't get caught, drugs are usually addictive, kill your precious brain cells, and do terrible damage to everyone around you.

For example, recently I read in the newspaper about a father whose son got hurt and needed legal drugs to help his injury. This father took some of his son's pills to test them and soon he was addicted to them. His son got better, but the father lied and said his son was still sick so he could keep getting the drug for himself. In just one year he took 2,286 pills. Eventually he got caught and he's now in jail. He was a student counselor at school and a town councilman. He lost it all just to take drugs.

We all hear stories like this every day in the media. We also hear about kids drinking alcohol, smoking cigarettes and pot, and worse. At some point we're going to have to decide what we're going to do when drugs are offered to us. But what do we really even know about what drugs are and how they mess with us?

Doctor, Doctor . . .

Most of what I know about drugs comes from the news—I'm no expert. That's why I decided to interview Dr. Whikehart for my chapter, since he is a psychiatrist and knows a lot about drugs and how people become addicted.

What Does "Abusing Drugs" Really Mean?

Doctor: Anytime a person takes a drug for any reason other than the one the drug was intended for, that person is abusing the drug. A good example of abusing drugs is when a doctor writes you a prescription of medicine to take away pain, but since it makes you feel good you take it even when you're not in pain. *(Sam: There are so many better ways to feel good without taking drugs—playing video games, hanging out with friends, playing ball.)* That's abusing the drug, because you're not taking it the way the doctor prescribed. When people take illegal drugs, that's abusing drugs too.

Why Do Kids Start Using Drugs?

Doctor: Because they're there. I think the most underestimated reason why people use and abuse drugs is their availability. If drugs aren't available, kids don't use them. If they are available, they do. I don't think people are any more likely to smoke pot because of peer pressure than they are to play baseball because of peer pressure. They play baseball because that's what their friends are doing and they do drugs because that's what their friends are doing. So, the best way to avoid using drugs is to avoid going to places where they will be available and avoid hanging out with other kids who use them.

How Addictive Is Marijuana?

Doctor: How addictive marijuana is depends on who is smoking it. Like many drugs, using marijuana feels different for each person. Some people find the drug's effects very exciting and thrilling, and some people find it frightening and scary. If a person finds the "high" frightening and scary, then it probably won't be very addictive for them. But if a person likes the "high," it will be much harder for them to stop smoking marijuana. They will easily become psychologically addicted to it.

The other bad thing about marijuana is that the chemical that makes you high stores itself up in your body. This means the withdrawal (getting drug free) may take months. If someone decides they want to quit smoking marijuana, they will have to be emotionally tough to do it. It's not easy.

What Effect Does Alcohol Have on Your Body?

Doctor: Alcohol is most notorious for killing liver and brain cells. It also kills the cells in the little capillaries that are at the ends of the arteries. That's why people who drink too much have red cheeks and red faces. The capillaries at the ends of their arteries have been killed. Actually, blood has leaked out or is constantly leaking out of the dead ends of the arteries. Alcohol is also a very addictive drug. *(Sam: Murdered capillaries and bleeding arteries! Gross, huh?)*

How Can I Tell if Someone Is Too Drunk to Drive?

Doctor: Police officers have what they call a "field test" to check if people are too drunk to drive. Alcohol affects the cerebellum, which is the part of the brain that handles coordination and balance and a lot of other things. So the test checks for problems with balance and coordination. If somebody can't walk straight and is clumsy, they're probably too drunk to drive. That's definitely the rule police officers use. Another thing the cerebellum controls is the tongue. If someone has slurred speech, it's probably safe to say he or she can't control a vehicle very well. If you see someone who isn't walking straight, seems uncoordinated, or is slurring words, you better call somebody to pick you up—that person is too drunk to drive.

(**Sam:** *Thousands of kids get injured or killed every year in drunk driving accidents. It's really not worth it to take a chance with your life if you think a driver is drunk.*)

I've Heard that Crack Is Really Dangerous— What Happens When a Person Takes It?

Doctor: Crack is a form of cocaine that people smoke or inject with a needle. It's an incredibly dangerous drug because it gets into your body and brain very quickly. When people snort cocaine, it takes about five minutes for the drug to hit the brain and make them "high." But if they smoke crack or use a needle (syringe) to inject it, the drug goes right into the bloodstream and the brain, and the "high" happens almost instantly. Crack users are able to get a lot more cocaine into their brains quickly, so it's much easier to get addicted and to overdose.

(**Sam:** *Lots of people die because of this drug. Recently a highly respected basketball player died from an overdose of crack cocaine. He was just out of college and expected to be a great star. Now that star will never shine.*)

If a Person Gets Addicted to Drugs, How Hard Is It to Quit?

Doctor: If a person is addicted to a drug, it means that drug is available to them. They can get the drug and they can abuse it. If that person can go to an inpatient rehabilitation center (a place where addicts live while they go through drug withdrawal), then the drug is no longer available to them. That makes it easier to quit and break the addiction.

If people can't do inpatient rehab then they have to keep themselves away from the drug, which is very difficult if they are addicted. Alcoholics Anonymous has a phrase, "People, Places, and Things," which means you can't hang out with the people you did drugs with, you can't go to the places where you did drugs, and all the things that remind you of drugs have to go. For instance, if you smoke cigarettes and really want to stop, you'd better not have cigarettes anywhere in the house or eventually you'll find them and light up again. So, if you're going to quit, you have to get away from the drug.

I also believe that it's easier to give up something if you get something else to take its place. People who are addicted to alcohol and join Alcoholics Anonymous have to give up alcohol, but they get a very solid support group with lots of new friends going through the same stuff they are. If you're going to give up drinking or doing a drug, it will be easier if you find another interest or hobby to take its place. Find something that makes you feel good in a healthy way to take the place of the addiction you're giving up. That's the best way to stop being addicted to a drug.

I'm Invited to a Party Where There'll Be Drugs and Alcohol. All the "Cool People" Are Going and I Want to Go Too . . . But I Don't Want to Do Drugs. How Can I Be Drug-Free Without Looking Like a Goody-Goody?

Doctor: What you really need to decide is whether or not you should go to the party at all. If you really don't want to do drugs, and you know that the reason most kids try drugs in the first place is because drugs are available, then going to a party where drugs are available would be a bad idea. Not going to the party would be the easiest way to avoid doing drugs. By not going to the party, you might be doing a lot of people a favor. There may be four or five people who change their minds and decide to skip that party because you decided not to go. Your bravery may be just the inspiration they need to avoid drugs also.

If you do go to the party, I think attitude is everything. If you look like you're unsure when you say "no" to someone offering you drugs or alcohol, you may be considered silly or uncool. But if your attitude says, "Hey, this is what's right for me and I'm not going to judge other people either," then you probably won't get too much pressure from your peers. Be firm and confident when you say "No, thanks" to people offering you drugs, but don't lecture everyone around you about what they're doing.

If alcohol is the issue, one easy way out is to just make yourself a "water cocktail." Put water and ice in a glass, squeeze some lemon into it, and you won't even have to deal with anyone teasing you for not drinking. They won't know what's in your glass and they won't care. Another thing that works is having all your reasons in your head about why you don't drink or do drugs, so when somebody starts to give you a hard time you can say, "Well, this is why I do what I do, and that's the way it is." Again, if you're confident about your decision, kids will usually respect it and leave you alone.

My Final Advice on Drugs

So, how come kids (and adults) still take drugs when they know drugs are bad for their health and are addictive? It could be because they want to be part of the "in" crowd. Or maybe they're tired of being pressured and pushed around by their friends. Fear of disapproval of your friends can cause you to do some pretty stupid things. If you're so afraid of losing your friends that you would risk your life to keep them, you gotta wonder if these are the friends you really want in your life. Be my friend and risk your life. Whoa! Think about it.

If you want to know more about drugs—what they are, what they do to you, how to avoid them, and how to help others who are hooked—look in the phone book for a local chapter of D.A.R.E. (Drug Abuse Resistance Education) or call D.A.R.E. national headquarters at 1-800-223-DARE. You can also check out its website at www.dare-america.com.

COOL COMEBACKS FOR STICKY SITUATIONS

OR HOW TO GET OUT OF A FIGHT WITHOUT GETTING TO KNOW THE PERSONAL LIFE OF THE SIDEWALK

Tucker Reda, age 12

✂ **Hobbies:** stunt biking, playing the bass and the drums
✎ **Favorite class:** music ✐ **Favorite authors:** Edgar Allan
Poe and Dr. Seuss ☹ **Pet peeve:** being ignored ♬ **Hero:**
Jimi Hendrix, John Lennon, Ringo Starr, and Alfred E. Neuman
❀ **Dream:** for my band to get famous, to own a Volkswagen bus,
and to travel

Bret Kuhl, age 12

✂ **Hobbies:** any sport on the planet, music, cards ✎ **Favorite**
class: math 📖 **Favorite book:** *The Contender* ☹ **Pet Peeve:**
doing the dishes ♬ **Hero:** Clyde Drexler and my dad ❀ **Dream:**
to play in the NBA

Do you ever get picked on? Do other guys make fun of your hair or your name? Do you always wish you had just the right comeback for those moments? Do you need something to say that would be funny, get them off your back, and protect you from getting clobbered?

We have gotten picked on a lot in the past and have learned that you've got to stay cool. We all know it's no fun to be picked on, but there are actually more creative ways to stand up for yourself than just arguing or getting in a fight. Here's our collection of useful disses, replies, stories, and advice on making a cool comeback in a sticky situation.

What Is a Dis?

A "dis" is when someone calls you a name, disrespects you, makes fun of you, or is rude to you. Disses are not a good thing. Disses are bad. They can lead to fights that result in you getting hurt, getting a referral, or even getting suspended from school. If a dis turns into a fight and gets really serious, it could lead to you getting expelled from school permanently and possibly even getting deported (foreign exchange students take note). If you get dissed, don't dis back. You don't want to sink to the level of the low-life who is dissing you. Therefore, you need to come back with a remark that is clever and funny—something that will make the low-lifes laugh and walk away, leaving you with the last word, all your limbs and your dignity intact.

Why the Heck Does Everybody Pick on Me?

Our theory is that since the beginning of time, people have picked on each other. Today this is still going on, but we are here to tell you some ways to get out of a sticky situation without getting to know the personal life of the sidewalk. We chose this topic because we are experts—we used to get picked on all the time (and sometimes even now). We believe that keeping your cool and talking your way out of a dis is better than fighting or telling on the disser. If you fight, you could get hurt, ruin your clothes, and get a bad reputation. If you tell on them, the word might get out that you're a real loser. It's sad, but it's true. Our advice is this: Outsmart them, make them laugh, and walk away. You win and no one gets hurt.

Top 10 Cool Comebacks for Getting Dissed

Here are our Top 10 comebacks that work for us. Give them a try—we think they'll work for you too!

Dis #1: Say you're short and someone disses you with "Hey Munchkin! You're so short, you belong in the *Wizard of Oz*!"

Your comeback: "Yeah, I was in that movie. I made a lot more money than you ever will."

Tip: If he keeps on dissing you after that fabulous remark, keep saying stuff like, "Yeah, yeah. I'm shorter than crud. Joy for me."

Dis #2: Say you're a little chubby and someone disses you with "Hey! You're so fat, when you pull up your BVDs, it says 'boulevard.'"

Your comeback: "Yeah, I'm a street. At least I'm useful, unlike you."

Tip: Keep your cool. Usually the person won't be such a blockhead and will walk away after a stunning comeback like that.

Dis #3: Say you're not the best looking guy in the world and someone disses you with "You're so ugly, Bigfoot takes pictures of you."

Your comeback: "At least Bigfoot notices me. He'd just step on you like another measly slug."

Dis #4: Say you've got a little acne and someone disses you with "Yo, acne face! Your face is so red it looks like the sun."

Your comeback: "Yeah, I'm the sun all right. I provide the Earth with warmth and solar energy. You provide the Earth with lame, sarcastic jokes that have been told and retold so many times they have lost all meaning."

Tip: Whoever is dissing you is probably just jealous because puberty is affecting you before them.

Dis #5: Say you've got a friend who's a girl and someone disses you with "Your best friend's a girl. Ha ha!"
Your comeback: "Yeah, you can learn a lot from girls. But at least I don't still talk to a sock puppet."

Dis #6: Say you have a space between your front teeth or a missing tooth and someone disses you with "You have such a big gap in your teeth, you look like Alfred E. Neuman."
Your comeback: "Yeah, I'm Alfred E. Neuman. I'm carefree. What, me worry?"

Dis #7: Say you have big ears and someone disses you with "You look like an elephant with those big ears."
Your comeback: "Yeah. I'm Dumbo. I can fly. You wouldn't want to be under a flying elephant when he's landing, would you?"

Dis #8: Say you're really tall and someone disses you with "How's the weather up there?"
Your comeback: "It's perfect. I get a lot of sun and the view is great. How's the weather down there, shorty?"

Dis #9: Say you're blonde and someone disses you with one of those incredibly stupid blonde jokes.
Your comeback (if they're a redhead): "Well, at least I don't look like a French fry with ketchup on it."
Your comeback (if they dyed their hair an odd color): "Well, at least it doesn't look like an animal got run over on my head."

Dis #10: Say you have braces like Tuck and someone disses you by calling you a "metal mouth" or "tin grin."
Your comeback: "Someday soon my teeth will be perfect and you'll still be dissing people to make yourself feel better. What a pity."
Tip: The point is to be creative, not mean. Hopefully the person dissing you will laugh hysterically and walk away after a comeback like one of these.

Replies for Lame Disses

Here's a dis that's as old as the hills, with a comeback that's as new as the millennium:

Lame dis: "You look like a four eyes with those glasses on."
Your comeback: A lame dis like that (or any other you might get) deserves a clever comeback like "You can dis me all you want about my glasses. Just give me something original. Call me when you get some new material."

Advice from Tuck for Drive-By Disses

If someone out of the blue, for no reason at all, sticks his or her head out of the window of a bus or car and flips you off or something, just stare at them like they are one of the biggest idiots on the face of the Earth. Never flip them back because you don't want to sink to their level.

Advice from Bret on Stumping Name-Callers

If someone comes up to you and calls you stupid or something, the first thing you should do is say, "Why do you do that? Don't you have anything better to do than call me names? Your life must be pretty boring if that's all you can think of.to do!"

A Story from the Real Lives of Bret and Tucker

Recently in our science class we were about to dissect our frog together. We had to name our frog, so we named it "The Mighty Mighty Spam Frog" after the band "The Mighty Mighty Bosstones." Then this annoying guy said that we were "gay" for naming our frog that. So we replied, "We are not gay for naming our frog after a cool band. You must not even know what the word means if you say that. Only a person with a low IQ wouldn't know what the word really means." He was so stumped that he sat down and didn't say another word.

We hope that you have enjoyed reading our chapter and that someday our advice will come in handy. And remember: Don't be one of those block-head dissers.

STAND UP FOR YOURSELF

Courtney Grant, age 13
✂ **Hobbies:** in-line skating, reading ghost stories and mysteries, playing football ✎ **Favorite class:** geography ✐ **Favorite author:** Stephen King ☺ **Pet peeve:** being teased or seeing others being teased ♪ **Hero:** Dr. Martin Luther King Jr. ❀ **Dream:** to become a famous journalist

Does This Scene Sound Familiar to You?

"Oh no! Let's hide! Here comes Kevin!"
"Courtney, get rid of Kevin. He's a geek!"
"Why do you hang around Kevin? He's a nerd!"
"Get lost! We don't want you hanging around us."

I chose this topic because so many boys, including me, are faced with this scene every day—kids being cruel to each other.

This cruelty has been directed at me for having a girl's name, for being African-American, for being overweight, and I've often watched it happen to others. I hate being pushed around and I also hate watching it happen to anyone else.

Over time I've learned how to stand up for myself in these situations and how to stand up for others who are getting picked on. Believe it or not, I've learned how to face these cruel situations with dignity, and you can too.

Why Do Kids Pick on Each Other?

I think kids (and people in general) pick on others because it gives them a sense of power. When you see someone harassing or putting someone else down, you'll find it usually happens in front of an audience. The bully is looking for attention and approval from his or her group.

Kids are often the most cruel to each other. They want to look cool or hip in front of their friends. If you take away a bully's friends, you'll have a defenseless rodent. (OOPS! I better watch my language.) Look at gangs, for instance. A gang isn't a gang if there's only one person. The kids in gangs are really just lacking love and seeking attention. Gangs provide the audience and the sense of belonging that insecure kids are looking for.

Stand Up for Your Rights

America's Declaration of Independence states that "All men are created equal, and are endowed with certain inalienable rights." This means that we are all equal and should have the same rights—rights that cannot be taken away by anyone. So, what gives someone the right to pick, push, or shove someone of weaker strength? What gives someone the right to use cruel words to batter another person's feelings? Is this right? My answer is no! We all have a right to be here. We are all pieces of a puzzle that fit snugly into this world. Nobody can be you or can take your place. Does it matter if your skin color, your size, your walk, or your voice is different? No. If we were all faultless, all the same, then we would miss out on beauty that comes from variety. We all need to begin respecting and protecting each other's differences.

How I Learned to Stand Up for Myself

I know how it feels to be teased. "Fat Slob," "Flat Nose," and "Big Lips" are names that were often thrown at me. They felt like poisoned darts aimed right at my heart. I used to get really angry and wanted to fight back against the people who teased me. Instead I learned how to reach out and grab those darts before they penetrated my heart.

Through my experiences, I've realized that people who tease others are really hungering for a sense of belonging and happiness, which they don't get at home. I started asking myself, "What's the use of fighting their emptiness with my anger?" Instead of fueling their hatred with my own anger, I tried pulling them closer by offering my kindness. Believe me, this isn't easy to do, but it can be done successfully. The lives of Martin Luther King Jr., Mahatma Gandhi, and the Dalai Lama show that you can handle conflict without resorting to anger and violence.

 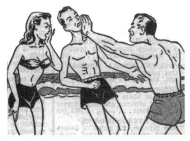 

Standing Up to My Tormentor

A few years ago I was getting picked on a lot at school. One kid in particular was really after me and never left me alone. His torture left me in total confusion. I couldn't think clearly. I couldn't concentrate on my school activities. He was ruining my life. But, instead of just giving up and taking it, I decided to do something about it.

With great embarrassment, I told my parents about my problems, about the verbal and physical abuse I was facing at school. It was one of the hardest things I've ever done. They listened patiently and when I finished pouring out my heart my mother softly whispered some surprising advice to me: "Courtney, if we were all created the same there would be no variety, no color, and no differences in the world. This world is full of envy, hatred, and cruelty and it's not going to change any time soon. You have to change.

Courtney, we love you so much, but you need to learn that it's not important to please others, it's only important to please yourself. Accept the things you cannot change and focus on changing the things you can. One of the things you can change is how you deal with your enemy. You can learn to love your enemy." I knew my mom was right.

The next day, as soon as I set foot inside the school building, the words "fat slob," "fat nose," and "big lips" were hurled straight at my heart. I could feel the blood racing to my head as anger started taking over. But instead of lashing out at the bully, I closed my eyes and saw my mom telling me, "You're better than this mud-slinger and you can handle him."

Before another piercing word could enter my heart, I reached out and greeted the bully with a handshake. With all the courage I could muster, I said to him, "Let's talk after class." I spent that whole class wondering what in the world I was going to say to him. My mind was a blank.

When the bell ending class rang, I still had no ideas. But sure enough the bully was waiting for me. To my surprise, I once again grabbed him in a firm handshake. I knew I had his full attention, so I hit him with a left hook of questions: "Why do you dislike me? What have I ever done to you?" I didn't even give him a chance to answer. I looked him directly in the eyes and said, "From this point on, we're going to be friends. If you ever call me another bad name, I'll go to the guidance counselor, principal, and assistant principal and demand that they have you and me to sit down one-on-one until we agree on a written plan of friendship. So, let's just make it easy for both of us and decide here and now to be friends. Agreed?"

I couldn't believe that I'd said all that. It felt great. But it felt even better when I heard him answer, "Agreed." And that was the end of my daily torture. He and I are not exactly the best of friends now (he's not the kind of person I'd want to be friends with anyway), but it's okay because I don't have to hear those negative words anymore. How you choose to stand up for yourself may be different from my story, but the key thing is to be honest and not be afraid of trying.

Standing Up for Others

There's a guy at my school named Kevin who always used to get teased. He's a great guy who happens to walk with a slight limp. During gym class he has a hard time controlling his muscles, which makes him look clumsy and off balance. You could always find Kevin sitting alone, being pushed around, or being called terrible names. He never defended himself—he just dropped his head and seemed to wish that he could disappear. I'm sure all of you out there know someone like Kevin. I don't understand what gives students the right to be so vicious to anyone! Everyone has his place in the world.

You know that old saying, "Sticks and stones may break my bones, but words can never hurt me." Well let me tell you, words not only hurt, they humiliate, embarrass, and destroy your self-esteem. Just being around Kevin when other students were cruel and mean to him hurt me deeply. I got so embarrassed for him and I knew that he must have felt left out and neglected. I had to do something—I couldn't just stand by and watch Kevin get abused.

I offered Kevin my friendship. I hung out with him when no one else would. If kids teased him in front of me, I hit them with my questions. The teasing started to happen less frequently. My friendship and support helped Kevin feel good about himself, and eventually he got the courage to stand up for himself.

How You Can Stand Up for Others

1) Try being a friend to someone who seems to need a friend—someone who may be going through a tough time.
2) Offer kindness instead of cruelty! Invite your new friend out on the weekends to play arcade games, go to the movies, go skating or even bowling. This is a great way to let people know that you like being with them and that they have a friend.

3) Share one of your favorite books with your friend. Trade creative ideas with one another.

4) Have the courage to let others see you with your newfound friend often, in spite of their negative comments. This is what being brave is really all about.

5) Finally, stand up for your friend when he is being harassed. I'm sure one day he will stand up for you!

Don't forget, feelings are fragile, delicate, and easily broken. Conquer peer pressure by being a true friend to all and I'm sure you will be sitting on top of the world. Remember, it's always nice to be nice. No one likes a bully.

More Advice on Standing Up for Yourself

Here are some questions that kids at my school gave me about their difficulties fighting peer pressure and trying to stand up for themselves:

Dear CJC,

I'm thirteen and my buddies are trying to force me to try smoking. They think they are so cool and grown-up because they smoke. I don't like smoking, but I do like my buddies. What should I do?

Signed, No Smoking Please

Dear No Smoking Please,

A classic case of peer pressure! Do you know the dangers of smoking? Do you know that it can kill you? Now, which is more important—your life or your friends? If you are smart (and I know you are) you will choose your life over your friends. Or perhaps I should call them your "so-called friends," because real friends would never ask you to do such a dumb thing. My advice to you is to stand up for yourself. Tell these friends that you don't want to smoke. If they tease you or keep pressuring you, find new friends who really care about you. You are young and have your whole life ahead of you. You don't need to start killing yourself just because other kids want you to.

Dear CJC,

My friends all think they're fly and cool because they wear the latest fashions—Tommy Hilfiger, Nike, Fubu—stuff like that. I want to be fly too, but my parents can't afford it. I'm too ashamed to tell my friends this. I want to hang out with them, but I'm afraid I'll lose their friendship if they find out I can't keep up with their fashions. What should I do?

Signed, Fancy Dresser

Dear Fancy Dresser,

Here we go again. Peer pressure has you bound. If these guys are your true, down-to-earth home boyz, they'll like and accept you the way you are and not for what you wear. After all, fashions are here today, gone tomorrow. So stand up for yourself and tell them the truth. See if they're your true friends or not. But if this advice doesn't satisfy you, try flea markets, thrift stores, and garage sales where there are lots of hip clothes at much more reasonable prices. Shop around. You can also put the big "C" in "cool" by earning your own money for clothes. You're old enough to mow lawns and do other odd jobs. So don't rely on your parents for everything. Good luck.

Dear CJC,

My mom won't let me go to the dances held at my school because she thinks they're not safe or properly supervised. My friends always go and brag about what an awesome time they have. How can I get my mother to change her mind?

Signed, Want to Dance

Dear Want to Dance,

Wow—tough problem! It sounds like you need to stand up for yourself with your mom. First, get a parent from the PTA (Parent Teacher Association) of your school to talk with your mom. The PTA often organizes these dances and makes sure they are safe. Second, I know most of us feel uneasy when our parents are around, but invite your mom to join the PTA and become a chaperone at your next dance. Then she can see for herself how safe it is and how much fun you have. Our parents may overprotect us when they don't know all the facts. So, get busy educating your mom and then have fun at the next dance.

My Final Words of Wisdom

This world is full of problems. Finding the answers is exciting and challenging. I'm not promising you a rose garden, but if you stand up for yourself and others in a peaceful, honest way, the world will be a much better place.

MAKE YOUR OWN TRADITIONS

Philip Taylor, age 13

⚡ **Hobbies:** basketball, soccer, skiing, traveling, being outdoors, and reading ☙ **Favorite class:** math and science 📖 **Favorite book:** *A River Runs Through It* ☺ **Pet peeve:** when adults interrupt what I'm saying and correct my grammar ✴ **Dream:** to live a long, healthy, and prosperous life

Andrew Manton, age 13

⚡ **Hobbies:** sports, skiing, traveling, and reading ☙ **Favorite class:** math 📖 **Favorite book:** The Redwall series ♪ **Hero:** my dad ✴ **Dream:** to be a writer

Do you get bored during Thanksgiving when the men watch TV and the women cook? Are your family vacations a chore with everyone fighting for what they want to do? Then this chapter is for you. We both come from families with very strong, fun, and unique traditions that we create together. These traditions make our holidays and vacations more fun for all of us. We probably take it for granted, but we think that guys like us should be able to experience holidays and traditions like we do. Take our advice and you'll get to be creative and invent traditions that are great fun for YOU and will lead to the best memories of your life.

So, What Is a Tradition, Anyway?

> **tradition** *n.* the handing down of statements, beliefs, legends, customs, etc., from generation to generation, especially by word of mouth or practice.

A tradition doesn't have to be something really technical, the way a dictionary describes it. In fact, traditions are all around you, whether you know it or not. In one family, a tradition might be going out to dinner every Friday night. Another group of people might hold an annual celebration on a certain holiday. Traditions come in all shapes and sizes—some are very simple while others are complex.

Traditions make life more interesting. Without them there would be nothing to celebrate. People around the world have built their cultures and communities around traditions. But it isn't only religious occasions or other holidays that make something a tradition. A tradition is really just something you do on a regular basis to celebrate. You can have traditions with your family, with your friends, even with your class at school. A tradition is what YOU do to celebrate—the activities you do, the ceremonies you invent, the memories you create, and the people you share them with.

Studies have shown that what people remember most about their childhoods are celebrations, parties, and things they do with their families, particularly holidays and vacations. These are the kinds of traditions that will help shape your life.

Anyone can start a tradition. It just takes effort, dedication, and creativity. The examples used in this chapter are based on our own family traditions. We happen to live with both our parents and close to lots of other family. But that doesn't mean you can't make your own family traditions if your parents are divorced or if you live far away from family. A tradition is just something you do over and over with people you love. So you can adapt our games, meals, and other celebrations to fit the people in your life who you would like to have traditions with.

Now that you know what traditions are, and how important they are, we're going to tell you some of our families' traditions to give you ideas and get you started.

The Fourth of July—Phil's Family Tradition

Our Fourth of July tradition was started by my dad's family when he was a kid and has been going on for nearly forty years! People travel from all over the country to come to our annual fiesta. All my dad's siblings come and most of them have kids of their own now, so it's a big party.

The whole celebration is kid-oriented, although everyone participates in the activities—from my 73-year-old grandfather, to some four- or five-year-olds. There's a softball game, egg and balloon tosses, sack races, and even a massive water fight. The water fight is traditionally started by the same person—75-year-old Dr. Gruber. Once he makes his first squirt gun attack there is a mad scramble for water weapons and balloons—an all-out water war!

The meal is classic: hot dogs, chips, etc., and, of course, dessert. Every year my aunt makes an American flag cake with blueberries and raspberries for the stripes. We sing songs and finish up the night with our own fireworks show—not one of those go-and-watch-the-big-fireworks shows but one of the little in-the-street kinds. Even though it's small, everybody loves it! We're disappointed when the day finally ends because we may not see some of the people for a whole year. But it is something we always look forward to.

Thanksgiving—Andrew's Family Tradition

What do most people do on Thanksgiving? The men sit and watch football while the women cook. Then they all eat a ton of food, watch TV for a while, and go to bed. It's very different at the Manton house. Our Thanksgiving day is based on togetherness—we cook, play games, do puzzles, and even tie-dye together.

There are some other things that make our Thanksgiving celebration unique. We leave our house open to anyone who wants to come, so I can't remember a Thanksgiving when we had less than twenty people there! We also split the day between two different houses: the "hang-out house" and the "dinner house."

There's always lots of fun stuff for kids to do. We kids get to make the Thanksgiving pies—we've been doing it since we were toddlers—even though we get covered from head to toe with dough. We laugh and scream . . . and eventually make pies. After dinner we go to the "hang-out house" for contests of wit and wildness. We play everything from Pictionary to "Sardines" (like hide-and-seek, but when people find the hider, they hide with him until the last person finds them all) to charades. The game we play doesn't matter. What really matters is that for those hours everyone in the room gets to be a little kid. Everyone goes home full, not just with Thanksgiving food but also with Thanksgiving spirit.

Christmas—Phil's Family Tradition

Christmas! The lights. The snow. The smell of Christmas trees. For the Taylor family, that's only part of it. This is the season of giving, and for us the giving isn't just to members of our family. Every year we do something for charity. One year we delivered food to our local rescue mission. Another time we adopted a family, giving them all the food they needed for a traditional Christmas dinner. Whatever it is we do, giving to others always makes Christmas mean more and makes us happier afterward because we've helped someone else.

In the days before Christmas, we sing Christmas carols with my grandparents, aunts and uncles, and other families. On Christmas morning we do the usual—open and play with presents and eat cinnamon rolls. Mmm-mmm! In the afternoon we get together with another family or go for a hike. Later in the afternoon my dad's side of the family shows up—grandparents, cousins, aunts, uncles—and we play our favorite game, "Who Am I?" In the game, each player has a sticker on his or her back with the name of a celebrity. You have to walk around asking other people yes-or-no questions to figure out who you are. Common questions are "Am I a guy?" or "Am I still alive?" After the game, we dig into a traditional turkey and ham dinner, with all of the trimmings. Everyone stuffs themselves to the maximum, only to realize that there's at least three pies to be eaten later!

The day is full of excitement with all sorts of fun things to do. But the important thing is that we spend the time together. Over the years this has become one of my family's richest traditions and each year it gets more and more fun.

Easter—Andrew's Family Tradition

Rain or shine, Easter is time for fun for the Manton family. Our first Easter tradition is our treasure hunt. This isn't just any old treasure hunt, but a hunt for all ages, with detailed maps and zany clues to follow. The candy treasure is buried or hidden in a washing machine or someplace secret but easy to get to. The clues are special because each one has something to do with the treasure hunter's life. If the hunter is learning Spanish, the clue may be in Spanish. If the hunter is into computers, the clue may be hidden in a computer. Each clue is difficult but also very fun to figure out.

Another favorite Easter activity is the egg juggle. It's not really an egg toss but more like egg chaos! To play, everyone stands in a circle and one person starts. The starter has an Easter basket filled with tons of plastic Easter eggs. The starter points to one person in the circle who they will throw to. Then that person points to the person who they will throw to, and so on, until you get back to the starter. Everyone in the circle should have one person they catch eggs from and one person they throw eggs to. Then the starter begins throwing the eggs, one by one, to their catcher. And that person throws to their catcher, and so on.

Soon eggs are flying everywhere! You play until you've dropped all the eggs or you're all exhausted from laugher! This is a great game because everyone is so focused on tossing and catching the plastic eggs that they totally forget their pride and just go all out—people of all ages grinning wildly, laughing, screaming, and having a grand old time.

Vacations—Andrew's Family Tradition

For vacations, especially travel vacations, compromise is the key to having a great time. Vacations are a time to relax and enjoy activities together, so everyone in the family should be in on the scheduling. That way your whole family isn't just doing what one person wants. During Manton family vacations there are always some activities that we all want to do and others that only some want to do. For example, often my parents want to take a hike but my sister and I just want to swim. So we compromise and do both activities for shorter periods of time. To make the trip more enjoyable, we all make small sacrifices.

One of our most important vacation traditions is our family quest for "the great swimming hole." Without it, our vacation is not complete. The water our family finds to swim in comes in all shapes and sizes—rivers, lakes, streams, oceans, and occasionally even pools—but no matter where we swim, we remember it later as paradise.

Vacations are great traditions because they're a break from everyday life, they're fun, and they build memories for the whole family. So find a place that looks exciting and start bugging your parents. And remember, vacations don't have to be expensive. They can be as simple as a camping trip in a nearby park or a day at the beach. Think your parents can't take you anywhere? How about setting up a tent in your own backyard? Wherever you take your vacation, have fun and be creative!

Backpacking and Camping—
Phil's Family Tradition

"Just a little farther," I tell myself, the twenty pounds on my back feeling more like two hundred.

"Dad, how far til we get there?"

"A little more than five miles," he says, as I go into a comatose state, wondering how in the world I'll ever make it.

Yes, backpacking can sometimes be like this, but in the Taylor family we hold an appreciation for the outdoors that helps us overcome such hardships. Backpacking and camping are about working together as a family to survive without the comforts of home. Not only do we get to appreciate the wonders of Mother Nature, but we also connect as a family in ways that are impossible back in our busy city lives.

My favorite camping tradition is the campfire, which we always build in the morning and again at night. The fire is where we gather to talk, tell stories, and sit quietly watching the flames.

But backpacking certainly isn't for everyone. One time we hiked for hours to a great campsite, only to have our camp stove break down. Since we had no other way to make dinner, we had to hike all the way back, racing out of the wilderness with a thunderstorm at our heels. These things happen, but they also make for your coolest stories and memories.

While camping is sometimes a hassle, doing it has helped me and my family see lots of beautiful sights. Our family vacations are my dad's favorite two weeks of the year. Who knows? You may enjoy it as much as we do.

Make Your Own Traditions

Now that we've given you examples of our favorite traditions, let's help you make some of your own. Here are our six easy steps to creating a home-made tradition.

Step #1: Get together with your family and talk about what holidays could use some more excitement, or refer to our list of holidays below. Choose one that the entire family agrees on and begin the process of livening it up. Be sure to involve each member of your family so everyone feels a sense of ownership in your new tradition. Have a discussion about the values your family would like to incorporate into your tradition. Remember how the Taylors give to charity at Christmas? Not everything has to be fun and games.

Step #2: Brainstorm and write down all sorts of activities and games that are appropriate for your celebration. These games are not set in stone, but they are good ice-breakers for your new traditions. Note: Be aware of weather conditions, depending on the time of year.

Step #3: List ideas for food and refreshments. Remember to include drinks, snacks, and desserts. Pick some family favorites that everyone will look forward to each year. Don't feel like you have to prepare them all by yourself. Encourage guests to bring treats of their own.

Step #4: Now is the time to decide on a specific time and place. Make sure it is a setting where there is room to play games and set up food. It could be at someone's house, in a park, at the beach, or even in a camp-ground. It should be somewhere that people are going to want to come back to year after year.

Step #5: Write down a list of all the people and families you wish to invite to your get-together. Then call or write invitations to all the people that you are inviting.

Step #6: One last thing—**HAVE FUN!!!**

Here are some holidays you could turn into fun traditions for you and your family:

SPRING

Easter, St. Patrick's Day, Cinco de Mayo, May Day (or Spring Equinox), Earth Day, Mother's Day, Memorial Day, Flag Day, Passover

SUMMER

Father's Day, Fourth of July, Labor Day, Rosh Hashanah, Summer Solstice

FALL

Yom Kippur, Columbus Day, Halloween, Veterans' Day, Thanksgiving

WINTER

Valentine's Day, Chanukah, Kwanzaa, Christmas, New Year, Martin Luther King Day, Groundhog Day, Chinese New Year, President's Day

And don't forget birthdays, anniversaries, and family reunions. These can all be excuses to create a new tradition.

Just remember to do your tradition every year so that it becomes a real tradition. And make sure it's fun for everyone. Go ahead and decide what you'll remember best about your childhood—then start making your memories now!

BEING THE BEST BIG BROTHER

Brandon Smith, age 10

✂ **Hobbies:** football, karate, reading, baby-sitting, and building models ✎ **Favorite class:** science and math 📖 **Favorite book:** *The Hobbit* ♪ **Hero:** Marc Edwards, my dad, and my poppy ❀ **Dream:** to be a naturalist when I grow up

There is nothing more fun or important to me than being a big brother. I love taking care of and playing with my baby brother, who is now a toddler. I picked this topic because there are lots of boys out there who have no clue how to take care of or have fun with a younger sibling. They just think it's a pain and don't see the good sides of it.

I think it is great having a younger sibling because he or she looks up to you and thinks you are one of the greatest people in the world. My baby brother already does all kinds of things that I do. I've shown him how to play ball, build block towers, do karate kicks, and make funny faces. I always get a big hug and a kiss as my reward. In my chapter you will learn the things that worked for me and my baby brother so you can actually have fun with yours. Remember: Being the best big brother you can be is a very important job and having a happy sibling makes life a lot easier and fun too.

Avoiding Baby Bloopers

Baby siblings go through many different stages. Each stage means you need to know different skills, there are different dangers to watch for, and there are different games and fun things you can do together.

Ideas for fun: Here are some things you can do to entertain your baby sibling from when he or she is a newborn until about eight months old.

☺ Smile and talk to them. You smile so they know you love them and to make them feel good. Sometimes babies will laugh when you smile and when you show love. Talking to them really helps the baby to get used to your voice. It is good to use a gentle and soft voice because otherwise, when they are older, they might be scared of loud noises.

☺ Reading to a newborn is very important. Reading is good because newborns will learn how to say sounds of letters and they will like the time and attention that you give them.

☺ Music can be soothing and entertaining. My brother always smiles and claps when he hears songs. You should play the music softly until your sibling is about a year old.

Skills needed: The first thing you should learn is how to hold your infant brother or sister correctly. Here's what you do: Cross your arms, then fold them down into the shape of a cradle. Then lift the right side of your arm-cradle a little bit higher than your left side, to support your baby sibling's head.

Dirty diapers . . . aaaah! This is a job that probably won't be your favorite. You should learn how to change diapers and help your mom or dad with this job, anyway. It's not that hard and you can learn how to do it by just watching your mom or dad and helping them out. First use diaper wipes to clean up your sibling's rear area. Then spread out the diaper under the baby and bring up the front flap. Use the sticky straps or safety pins to stick it together. Make sure you check that his/her rear end is in the diaper. One time I didn't check and my baby brother ran around with half his rear hanging out! Oh, and you better hurry if you're changing a baby brother because he will pee all over you if you don't.

Baby Safety Tips:

1) Don't let babies play with anything really small. They may choke on it.

2) Don't let babies near anything sharp or pointy. They could get cut.

3) Be careful when you pick babies up and hold them. They are very fragile.

4) Don't let babies near anything that is hot. You need to teach them the difference between hot and cold.

5) Don't leave babies close to water. They could drown in just a small amount of water.

6) Always behave yourself in front of babies so that they learn to behave correctly too. Babies will imitate everything you do—good or bad.

Creeping Crawling Sibling

Ideas for fun: The next stage is from about eight months to two years old. Here are some fun things that I did with my brother.

☺ Try to teach them how to crawl when they are eight or nine months old. One way of doing this is to put a favorite toy on the floor and get on all fours like a baby. Then start to crawl toward the toy. The baby will begin to try this idea of crawling by imitating you.

☺ Playing together with blocks is fun. When your younger sibling gets to be older and starts crawling, you can build up boxes or blocks into a pyramid or tower. My brother likes this game a lot. I stack them up and then he knocks them down. Also, it teaches babies to entertain themselves.

☺ Teach babies how to talk. I like to read to my brother and say words like "mama," "dada," "bra," "ba-ba," " yes," and "no." Why say those kinds of words? So babies can try to say those words and learn the sounds of letters.

Time for Some Action

Ideas for fun: When a sibling is between one and two years old you can start playing some more active games.

☺ Play peek-a-boo. Kids this age really love the peek-a-boo game because it is fun and they like the attention that you give them.

☺ Ride siblings around in a wagon if you have one. They like the wagon because they enjoy moving around kind of fast. But don't go too fast because they could fall out and hurt themselves. When they get hurt and cry, it is one of the most horrible feelings in the world for a big brother!

☺ Giant birds and purple dinosaurs. This age is a good time to introduce siblings to something that is nerve-racking to us older brothers, but young siblings usually really like it a lot. One is big and purple and the other is tall and yellow. They are Big Bird of Sesame Street and Barney. I know you are probably freaking out, but all little kids love them both. It also keeps them busy and gives you time to yourself.

More safety tips: At this age many of the safety tips for young babies still apply, but a few new ones should be added.

1) Don't let them near stairs or windows. They could fall.
2) Never let them play with matches or near fire. My brother seems to be fascinated with the fireplace.
3) Keep doors and cabinets locked and closed at all times. Kids could get into poisonous fluids and drink them or spray them in their eyes.
4) Don't let them near any poisonous plants or animals.
5) Don't leave them alone for any reason. They are very curious and will probably find trouble.
6) Keep your bedroom door closed so they don't get hurt playing with your stuff. Then they can't break your stuff or mess up your room either.

Totally Toddlers

The toddler stage starts at about two years old. This can be a tough stage for you because two-year-olds may want their own way all the time, and sometimes they scream and yell a lot.

Skills needed: One of the first things you should learn to do is to relax and keep a smile on your face. Things will get better soon. They can't stay this age forever, can they?

Ideas for fun:

☺ Help them learn to talk. At this age they start to talk in sentences, and they need all the help they can get.

☺ Read more stories together. As they get older, your younger brother or sister will like to read stories with you even more than before. Reading together will help them develop better speech and a bigger imagination.

The types of stories I read to my baby brother are ones with Barney or Sesame Street characters in them. I read those to him because he loves to look at the pictures and listen to what his favorite characters do. When I read to him, he sits on my lap and he listens to the story. I use silly voices and act out what the book is saying. I know he really likes it because when I am done with one book, he puts it away and comes back with another one.

☺ Play some ball. Sometimes it is fun to kick or throw a ball with your baby brother. We play with a big rubber ball or a wiffle ball. I throw it and then he goes after it. Whenever you kick a ball, be careful not to kick it too hard because the ball may hit your brother.

My favorite game to play with my little brother is football. We chase each other, I tackle him (very gently), and he tries to tackle me. I taught him to spike the ball down and put his arms straight up in the air over his head, like the referees do, and then I yell "Touchdown!" My brother gets so excited that he looks like he just won the Superbowl.

☺ Hide and seek is a good game to play because when they find you they start laughing hysterically because they think it is real funny.

Your Future as the Best Big Brother

Remember—during all of these stages you need to love your younger sibling very, very much. There are a lot of boys that really want to have a baby brother or sister but don't get to. I had to wait a long time for my brother, so I know how it feels. Those of us who finally get them are pretty lucky. Even if they sometimes drive you crazy, be thankful for your sibling. I've learned that with a lot of patience and love you can get through almost anything, and even have a great time. Now that you know all of my ideas, have fun and be the best big brother ever!

THE BOYS' MOVEMENT

Justin Skord, age 12

✂ **Hobbies:** writing, juggling, acting, karate, playing piano, basketball, baseball, and skiing ✎ **Favorite class:** social studies 📖 **Favorite Book:** *The Lion, the Witch and the Wardrobe* ☹ **Pet peeve:** when I have to get horribly long lectures from my parents ♫ **Hero:** Ross Perot ❀ **Dream:** to become a great writer, actor, or politician

Have you ever read magazine articles declaring how great it is and how much courage it takes for girls to go out and join a boys' sports team? Or how about headlines that celebrate girls acting tough like boys. But who cheers for the boy who wants to learn how to dance or cook, or who cries during sappy movies? Most likely it's not his parents, his cousins, his grandparents, the press, the magazines, or anybody else a boy looks to for advice these days.

Now, before you jump to conclusions, I want you to know that I am not against girls getting encouragement for doing "boy things." In fact, I am totally for girls doing any activities they want. Hey, it's a free country! But I think people forget about the boys. It's not that easy for us either. There is a lot of pressure not to do "girl things"—maybe even more pressure than girls face now.

I decided to write this chapter because a few years ago I really wanted to join a choir. I love to sing, but I faced some major teasing for wanting to do this "girl activity." This experience inspired me to write about how we guys are also affected by stereotypes and how we need to fight it and start our own "boys' movement," like the girls have been doing.

Stereotypes

Practically all of you have heard the word "feminism," but have you ever heard the word "guyism"? Probably not. How about "girl power"? Do bands sing about "boy power"? I doubt it. I think that's because it's taken for granted that boys have all the freedom and options in the world. Everybody thinks girls have it harder in this life because they are sometimes smaller and weaker, and in many ways their choices can be limited. Everybody thinks we boys are free to do whatever we want. But the truth is we are all limited by stereotypes.

One of the things I have noticed and other people I interviewed have noticed is that there is some major stereotyping going on in this world today. "Stereotype," in this instance, means to generalize about what a girl likes and what a boy likes. Some of the most common stereotypes we all grow up with are:

Girls like pink and boys like blue.
Girls like horses and boys like cars.
Girls like Barbie and boys like G.I. Joe.
Girls are overly emotional and boys never cry.
Girls like to act, dance, and sing,
and boys just like sports.

What Is C.M.S.S.?

C.M.S.S. stands for "Chronic Male Stereotyping Syndrome." I've invented a test that will let you see whether or not you have been a victim of C.M.S.S. or have noticed it in your life.

Do You Have C.M.S.S.? Take the Test

1. Have you ever made fun of another boy because he did an activity like dancing, singing, acting, or gymnastics?
2. Have you ever chickened out of doing something you really wanted to do because you thought people would tease you?
3. Have you ever tried something new, just to quit right away because it was mainly girls doing it?
4. Have you ever made fun of an activity that only girls do?
5. Do you ever feel like you can't express your feelings if it means showing affection, sadness, or fear?

That wasn't so hard, was it? If you only answered yes to one or two of these questions, you're doing okay. You should read on to learn more about how to fight stereotypes and do what you really enjoy. But, if you said yes to three or more of these questions, that means you are a victim of this horribly fatal syndrome (just kidding about the fatal part). Seek help immediately by reading the rest of my chapter right now.

My Experience with C.M.S.S.

A few years ago, I had my own brush with stereotypes and the dreaded C.M.S.S. As I mentioned earlier, in the fourth grade I really wanted to join my school choir. But I knew that if my classmates found out, they would call me a sissy and worse. So I didn't even think about joining. I gave up my dream.

When the fifth grade came around I decided I should at least see if I liked choir. When I went to check out the first rehearsal I had never seen so many girls and so few boys in my entire life. So what do you think I did after that? I bolted from the room. And I still didn't join the choir.

In the sixth grade I still wanted to sing, so I finally said to myself, "You're going to join the school choir whether you like it or not!" I went back to the same choir room I had been in a year ago, and again there were girls as far as the eye could see, and no boys in sight. But this time I stood my ground. The music teacher greeted me in a friendly, welcoming manner. At first I felt a little uncomfortable, but as the practice went on I began to do what I really like to do—sing.

Soon kids found out about my C.M.S.S. ordeal and a few made fun of me. At first, I have to say, the teasing got to me. I even considered quitting the choir, after all I had been through. In the end though, I decided that since I had struggled to get this far, I might as well say to heck with those kids who want to make fun of me. It's not my problem, it's theirs. If they want me to reroute my life so that I'm not in the choir, too bad.

Eventually, those kids laid off teasing me. I ignored them and I think they realized that I didn't care what they said about me. I wasn't going to quit choir. Also, I began enjoying singing so much that their opinions meant nothing to me. Getting over C.M.S.S. and joining choir encouraged me to try other activities that I enjoyed. Last year I even signed up for a summer drama camp.

It seems like lots of kids are obsessed with making fun of other kids who just want to do something they enjoy. I don't believe that singing in choir makes me a sissy. As far as I'm concerned, I'd rather be a part of the group that's brave enough to be different and do what they really want to do.

Our Dads Fought C.M.S.S. Too

I was wondering how long this Chronic Male Stereotyping Syndrome has been around, so I asked my dad if he ever experienced it. He told me that when he was a kid, boys didn't even think about joining "girl" activities. Back then the rule for being a boy was to act like you didn't care about getting good grades or doing extracurricular activities. Enjoying school and being in nonsport activities wasn't "cool." Guys tried to get out of school as fast as they could, as soon as the bell rang.

In elementary school, my dad pretty much followed the so-called rules of being a boy: He got bad grades, played sports, and didn't even think about joining other activities. But in high school he began to realize that there were other things he liked to do. It was time to ignore what everyone else did. So he learned to play guitar and even started doing better in school.

My dad regrets that he let other guys dictate his life as a boy. If he could go back in time, he would have joined more activities and he would have had more fun in school. My dad believes that if you are not doing what you like to do right now, you better get on it. Don't let C.M.S.S. scare you away. Ten or fifteen years from now you'll wish you had gone for it.

Even Our Grandfathers Battled It

Just how far back does C.M.S.S. go? It turns out that even my grandfather had to struggle with the "disease." He always felt different from other boys his age. He never understood why they were always comparing how strong they were and competing against each other in sports. When he was about ten years old, his father put him on a baseball team, which he wasn't too excited about. While playing in the outfield, he suddenly realized, "Why am I sitting out here, waiting for the ball to fly to me so I can catch it and feel good about myself? Well, sorry, but that just doesn't amuse me at all. Even if I win, I don't think that makes me better than the other team. So what's the point?" He left baseball and other sports for good.

My grandfather liked other activities more than sports. He had a great

imagination and liked to make up his own games. He concentrated on doing things he truly liked to do. Even though he wasn't much of an athlete, my grandfather was still elected president of his class and was pretty popular.

It just goes to show you that if you stick with your real interests and do the things you want to do, things will turn out okay and people will respect you for being who you really are. All of us have something that makes us unique, but many people are afraid to show it. I admire my grandfather because he knew what he wanted to do and did it without questioning himself. That takes a lot of courage.

How to Recover from C.M.S.S.

Okay, if you answered yes to three or more questions in the C.M.S.S. test, here are some ideas and hints on how to recover from your case of C.M.S.S.:

1) Grab two pieces of paper and on one make a list of what you really like to do. After that, make a list on the second piece of what you're doing right now in your life. The key thing here is, if there's something on your "like to do" list and not on your "what you're doing now" list, you should ask yourself is it because of stereotyping? Am I afraid to do it because of C.M.S.S.? Like my dad, you may need to change activities.

2) Talk to men or other boys who have recovered from C.M.S.S. You might try your dad, grandfather, or uncles. Look for boys your age who are singing, dancing, acting, and doing other "girl" activities. Find out how much teasing they get and if doing what they really want is worth it to them.

3) Convince a friend to join your activity with you and be a "renegade" (someone who is independent, an individual, a nonconformist, a maverick, a radical).

4) Do some research and make a list of famous men who have made a name for themselves doing what you get teased for. If you like to sing, look at the lives of some famous rock stars. If you want to paint, check out some famous artists. If you love acting, get to know the pasts of your favorite movie stars. Was it always easy for them? Did they get made fun of by their peers. Was it worth it for them in the end?

5) Always remember the famous quote by Albert Einstein: *"Great minds don't think alike. They think for themselves."*

How to Prevent C.M.S.S. in the First Place and Be a Part of the "Boys' Movement"

Here are some ideas on how to prevent C.M.S.S. from taking place, if you don't already have it:

1) Show the world who you really are. Don't allow other people's judgments to change who you are. You know more about yourself than anyone else does, anyway.

2) Express your true beliefs and be brave with your opinions. For example, you could start a class project examining stereotypes. Your class could look for stereotypes in magazines, books, TV shows, movies, music, etc.

3) Once you know where the stereotypes are coming from, boycott (don't buy) those magazines, books, TV shows, movies, music, etc.

4) Show your feelings. Why can girls cry, be scared, and hug each other, but guys can't? Think about how dumb it is that guys aren't allowed to feel things that are just part of life. Don't be afraid to show your true emotions, even when you think it's "girly." That's what true bravery is all about!

5) Convince some guy friends to form a Renegade Club with you—perfect for guys who want to do their own thing, not just what stereotypes tell them.

6) Support other guys who are fighting C.M.S.S. (bands, athletes, artists, friends). Cheer on all these renegades.

7) Always be yourself!!! And remember that you aren't the only person on Earth going through this.

Conclusion

I'm proud to write about this little-known problem and to let people out there know what we boys are going through. You might not think it looks cool now to act, dance, sing, or do other "girl" things, but hopefully you've learned enough from my chapter to know that you will regret it when you're thirty years old if you never try. Don't let C.M.S.S. dictate your life. And spread the word. This could be the beginning of our own "guy power" movement.

YOU & YOUR PALS

MAKING FRIENDS & KEEPING THEM

Max Wojtanowicz, age 13

✂ **Hobbies:** academic triathlon, speech, band, choir, reading, piano, writing, theater, singing, swimming

✎ **Favorite class:** choir, English, geography

✐ **Favorite author:** Stephen King ☹ **Pet peeve:** when people think they are better than other people

♫ **Hero:** Andrew Lloyd Webber and George Winston

✺ **Dream:** to succeed in all that I do

"What should my topic be?" I thought to myself. My pencil was chewed almost in half and my eraser was entirely gone, since I'd had so many stupid ideas already. Five Mello Yellos and four Pixi Stix later, I gave up in frustration. How was I supposed to think of a topic that would stir the emotions of boys across the nation? A topic that's important to all living souls on the planet? So, I did the only thing possible in such an intense situation. I picked up the phone and called my best friend.

As I waited for her to pick up, I realized, "Hey! That's my topic!" Friends are just about the most important thing on Earth, but sometimes they're hard to make and keep. Hopefully my experience with friends will help you make the right friendship choices.

Making Friends

I walked into the huge theater and thought, "Everyone here is going to be a better actor than me. I'm going to be terrible and they're going to hate me. I don't know anyone . . . how am I going to make any friends?"

It was the first day of practice for "You're a Good Man, Charlie Brown" and I had the lead role. I walked nervously into the practice area of the theater and saw that most of the cast was already there. I took a seat and looked around at all the unknown faces. It was only a twenty-person cast, but that day it seemed like a hundred. This was going to be tough.

I learned a lot about making new friends that day.

☆ When you meet new people, remember that first impressions are important. Don't be shy; greet people enthusiastically. Then they will all remember you as fun and interesting.

☆ Don't be the only one talking, but don't be the only one not talking, either. Try to join in conversations, especially with new people.

☆ Ask people questions and listen to their answers. Learn more about them and try to find out if their interests are anything like yours.

☆ Try not to exclude anyone from the conversation. They might get the idea that you're selfish or rude.

Later in the rehearsal, I got really thirsty. I asked the group I was talking with if anyone had a water bottle, and a tall, dark-haired girl gave me hers.

"I'm Alison. I'm gonna play Lucy," she said. From that day on she's been my best friend. And that brings up another great point about making new friends:

☆ Offer something to someone. It doesn't have to be anything spectacular, just a little something that could make their day better.

Keeping Friends

Alison and some of my other friends have helped me to learn how to be a better friend. Some of the ways to be a good friend that I find most helpful are these:

☆ Go to social gatherings. Notice how I didn't say "parties" because that's not necessarily what I'm talking about. It could be a sports event, a movie, a dance, whatever. You'll meet new people there and learn to build better relationships.

☆ Don't let your friends pressure you into going to a party or something you feel weird about. Remember, it's your choice whether you want to go or not. Maybe whoever is hosting the social gathering has a bad reputation around school, or maybe you just don't like them, and that's okay. You don't have to go anywhere you don't want to.

☆ Keep your promises. This may sound simple, but it can actually be tough once you think about it. Don't use the phrase "I promise" unless you really do. Promising includes paybacks, showing up at places at the right times, etc.

☆ Don't tease your friends. It's okay to do it as long as you know you won't hurt their feelings. But if you do hurt their feelings, then you have a real problem. If you don't apologize quick, they might:

a) take it the wrong way, and it could hurt more than you intended it to.

b) hold a grudge against you.

c) spread rumors.

d) ditch you altogether.

e) all of the above. Ouch!

Of course, if your friends are hurting you with their teasing, they probably aren't worth having. Look at it this way: Take a sheet of paper; this is you. Rip it in half; the rip is the insult. It hurts, doesn't it? It's also hard to get the paper back to its original state.

Finding the Right Friends

I asked a lot of people what they see as the ideal friend. Their idea of a good friend is someone who is:

caring, sensitive, kind, wise, bright, clever, honest, loyal, trustworthy, agreeable, helpful, supportive, compassionate, easygoing, understanding, a good listener, confident, fun to be with, outgoing, and friendly.

I also asked what makes a bad friend. They said someone who is: *unfriendly, boring, greedy, close-minded, annoying, unkind, irresponsible, unfair, hardhearted, a user of chemicals, selfish, lazy, and a smart-aleck.*

Keep in mind that just because someone is something "good," like smart, funny, or good-looking doesn't mean that they would automatically make a good friend for you.

Fitting In

When I started junior high, I was overwhelmed by all the new people in my new school. I live in a pretty small town, and when you go from an elementary school of about 90, to a junior high of about 260, things get a little more stressful. But I could tell right away what the cliques were and who was in them.

In most schools, there are obvious cliques that stand out. In my school there are three: the popular people, the mediocre people, and the not-so-popular people. You can tell each group from the other. For example, popular people usually wear the nicest clothes, have certain hairstyles, or something like that.

There are probably these and many more cliques at your school. Trying to fit yourself into one of these cliques can be pretty painful. It's better to try to find people who enjoy what you enjoy and have the characteristics you're looking for in a good friend, instead of putting yourself in a group you don't necessarily like just to be popular.

One thing you should never (and I mean never) do is try to change yourself for other people. It's all right to change an interest or add a new one, but when it comes down to changing your personality, that's where you should draw the line. Changing your clothes, your hairstyle, getting lower grades, and losing the respect of the people around you are certainly not things you want to shoot for. People should like you for who you are, and not for what you wear or do.

Max's Friendship Bill of Rights & Privileges

This is probably the most important part of this chapter. As a friend, you have certain rights that your friends need to take into consideration, and a privilege that you need to try and keep.

☆ **You have the *right* to free speech.** You can express your opinions (as long as they don't offend or hurt someone) without anyone harassing you about these views. You have the freedom of speech, religion, and everything you want to express, no matter what anyone else thinks. If others can't accept you for who you are, then they obviously don't know how to be a good friend.

☆ **You have the *right* to listen** to your friends' opinions and not harass them. Obviously, it has to go both ways.

☆ **You have the *right* to say "no"** to anything you don't want to do. Remember, if a friend pressures you to do something that makes you feel uncomfortable, he or she is probably not worth having as a friend.

☆ **You have the *right* to be yourself.** You don't need to transform into somebody's duplicate. You are your own person and nobody needs a copy of someone else. If you want that, get a clone.

☆ **You have the *privilege* to be trusted.** You can lose this privilege pretty quickly if you're not careful. What if someday you're walking along the hall and you stop to talk to Joe or Bob or whoever, and you tell them that really big secret your best friend told you not to tell anyone? Big mistake! Trust is a fragile thing and it's hard to gain back once you lose it.

It All Comes Down to the Three Rs

Okay, this chapter is almost done. I hope you've learned a lot about how to make new friends, be a good friend, and keep your privileges to hang out with them. But all you really need to know are the three Rs:

RESPECT · RECONCILE · REMAIN

RESPECT your friends' rights and privileges. This is the best way to build strong friendships.

RECONCILE when you fight with your friends. Be honest about your feelings and admit your mistakes. Then try to resolve the problem. This is how you build lasting friendships.

REMAIN true to yourself. Don't change your personality for anyone. If people are friends with who you're pretending to be, then they're not friends with the real you. What's the point?

Of course, real life is bound to be a little more complicated than this, but these are the basics. These are the three friendship rules you'll need all your life.

DO THE "WRITE" THING

Justin Bailey, age 15

✕ **Hobbies:** R/C cars and airplanes, water skiing, writing, playing the saxophone ✕ **Favorite class:** concert band 📖 **Favorite book:** *Star Wars: The Last Command* ☹ **Pet peeve:** school ♫ **Hero:** Harrison Ford ✸ **Dream:** to be a pilot

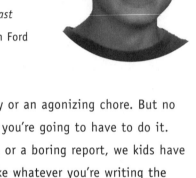

Creative writing can be an exciting hobby or an agonizing chore. But no matter what, it's a fact of life that at school you're going to have to do it. Whether it is a fun and creative writing idea, or a boring report, we kids have to write. The trick is using good skills to make whatever you're writing the best it can be. That's what this chapter is about. Anyone can write a good story if they are motivated. Even you!

Coming Up with Cool Concepts

I write because sometimes I'll get a really cool idea that I just can't pass up. I get ideas everywhere—from movies I see, places I go, and experiences I have. It's important to write about things you know. I love to read adventure, horror, and science fiction books, so those are the kinds of stories I write. There are other kinds of creative writing though: mysteries, historical fiction, Westerns, romances, etc. The possibilities are endless. Write in the style that you know and love.

But what if you can't think of any ideas? If that happens, don't let it get to you. Here are some good strategies for coming up with ideas and getting in the writing mood:

1) Think of topics that you like: sports, hanging out, movies, or girls. If you like sports, write a sports story. If you like hanging out with friends,

write a story about hanging out with friends—hey, that topic could even be an entire TV sitcom.

2) If you're stuck for ideas, try thinking of other stories that you've read and build on them. You could write an alternate ending to the story. Or you could write a sequel or a new, unique story using the same characters or the same setting.

3) Do the same thing with a movie. Pick your favorite movie and try writing your own sequel. I'm currently working on my own sequel to *Star Wars*.

4) If you can't think of a good movie, go see one. Sometimes the best time to write is after watching a good movie. An action flick might give you an idea to write a story about your favorite action hero foiling an international terrorist's horrendous scheme. The same goes for books—if you can't think of a good book, go read one. You'll get lots of ideas while reading someone else's writing. Jot your ideas on a piece of paper as you read, so you don't forget them.

5) If none of these tips work and you're still stuck for ideas, consider finding a quieter place to write. If you're trying to write in a noisy, crowded, or distracting place, chances are you'll never think of your best ideas.

Don't Worry if It's Weird

The next thing you need to do is keep that good idea interesting for yourself as well as the reader. The more interested you are, the more interesting your story will turn out to be. Even if the idea is far-fetched or even downright weird, you shouldn't be afraid to write about it. When I was younger I wrote a story about how some famous cartoon characters went on strike because they felt they weren't getting paid enough. It was a pretty bizarre story, but I ended up getting a great grade on it.

Just because the idea sounds weird doesn't mean it will make a bad story. Staying open to just about anything is the best approach. Sometimes building upon other stories or real situations can make it interesting. For example, the Unabomber decides to bomb his own trial or the Empire in *Star Wars* attacks Earth. These are good ideas that could make some interesting stories. The important thing is to keep an open mind to interesting ideas. Don't talk yourself out of them.

Creating Characters

A big problem can happen before you even begin to write your story. Sometimes people have trouble creating characters. This can be solved in a fairly simple way. In a good-versus-evil story, think of who you consider the ideal hero: a take-charge guy (or girl) with the brains of a genius and the brawn of a world-class weight lifter. Or your hero doesn't have to be tough or smart. He could be a zero who turns into a hero. You could make your bad guy the mirror image of your worst enemy, with even *more* bad traits.

After you have your main characters thought out, it's a good idea to add supporting characters to the list. They can be like the main characters, or not quite as smart or strong as the heroes or villains. The possibilities are endless, just choose what interests you the most and move your story along.

Starting Your Story

Sometimes people think they need a lot of things to begin writing: a fancy computer, a great notebook, or the perfect idea. But really, the only tools you need are something to write with (a cheap pencil and a pad of paper work fine) and your imagination.

It's usually best to think out your story before you start writing. You can think it out in your head or write down ideas and an outline on paper. I'm actually pretty bad about that. Sometimes I write the story as I go along and play it by ear. I often get really stuck when I try to do it all in my head. It can take longer to write an outline, but it will probably help you later when you don't know where your story's going and you get "writer's block."

Breaking "The Block"

Have you ever sat down to write something, but nothing comes into your brain? Nothing! That's "writer's block" and it can be your worst enemy. Here are a few tips to fight it:

1) Go back and change the story a bit. Having a new twist may help get the story flowing again. It's sort of like saving your progress in a video game. If you mess up, you can go back to the last good part of the level and do the messy part over.

2) Take a break from your story and come back to it later. Do something else, like watch TV, read a book, see a movie, or go for a walk. Usually, taking your mind off your story will help new ideas pop into your head. You can go back to your story with a clear head and fresh ideas.

3) Sleep on it. Sometimes you'll get ideas from your dreams.

4) Put it away for a while. Sometimes I tuck stories away in my drawer (especially the ones that I think are really bad) and read them again a few months later and get a good laugh. But sometimes I get more than just a good laugh. Reading an old story sparks new ideas that I can write another story about. Often I finally finish the old story too.

Above all, don't get discouraged with stories you're not pleased with. It happens. Don't give up on them. You just have to bounce back and stay motivated.

Penning the Perfect Plot

Story flow is another important aspect. A story without a good plot is quickly tossed aside by the reader. The plot is what holds the reader's attention. Establish your plot early and don't skip around from scene to scene without a good reason. Otherwise, you may be leaving your readers in the dark until the very end, when your story wraps up like a "Mission Impossible" episode.

"Mission Impossible" did have one great quality about it—suspense! Good suspense will leave the reader hanging on your every word until the very end. It's like playing a game of "I-know-something-you-don't-know." Readers want to find out what it is, but you only give them a few clues at a time. If you master this style, you could have a great career writing suspense novels. The trick is to reveal just a little bit at a time, just enough to keep the readers hooked. Keep building your story until they're biting their nails. Then, when you throw the climax at them, you'll get a good "Wow!"

Devising Dynamite Dialogue

An important thing to work on when writing a story is good back-and-forth dialogue. Dialogue keeps the story flowing and moves the plot along, so it's important to keep the dialogue smooth and interesting. This isn't as easy as it sounds at first.

One thing to avoid is using the word "said" too much. Here's an example:

"Great catch!" said the coach.

"Thanks!" said the player.

"You're an awesome player," said her teammates.

As you can see, this kind of dialogue gets tiresome and boring pretty quickly. Instead, use words like "cheered" or "asked" or "repeated." If the dialogue is between just two people, you can write the dialogue without having to say who said what.

As I mentioned earlier, I've been inspired by the *Star Wars* movies to write my own sequels. Here is an excerpt from one that I'm working on that has some good back-and-forth dialogue:

"Raise shields! Charge the turbolasers!" barked General Straits, as a devilishly greedy grin crossed his face.

The com officer stood up in his seat, raising an eyebrow.

"Sir, it is Standard Imperial Procedure to notify command of unidentifiable spacecraft."

"DO AS I SAY!" *yelled the general, walking toward the young recruit. "It is also Standard Imperial Procedure to throw a disobeying officer into the brig!"*

Shakily, the officer whined, "Understood, sir. I apologize for my independent judgments."

As you can see, it's possible to describe what the characters are doing while they're talking. This technique lets the reader visualize the setting and makes the story more interesting.

Grappling with Guidelines

The hardest thing for me about creative writing is following guidelines, especially the ones that come from school assignments. Teachers tell you, "The story has to be two to four pages long" or "It has to be about this, this, and this." With too many guidelines, my creative thinking is squandered and I end up limited to just a few ideas. That can make anyone turn in some really lame material.

One school assignment I had was to design a country, which wasn't a problem until I learned about all the guidelines. I had to write a folk tale about my fictional country, but since I had chosen to create a futuristic country, I wasn't prepared for a folk tale. What made matters worse was that the folk tale had to be shorter than four pages. The story I had in mind was supposed to be a long epic. I ended up having to shorten it considerably, but there wasn't much I could do about it.

To Make a Long Story Short

If you get into a situation like mine, where you have to shorten your writing, you can leave out lengthy parts that don't help the plot move along. You can also summarize in a short paragraph the part you left out.

Here's an example. Instead of writing all the action and dialogue in a battle scene, write a paragraph that just tells the reader what happened in the battle:

Thousands of soldiers were killed in the battle for the small island. In the end, the revolutionists won control and began deciding their own destiny.

Be sure to leave in crucial points of the plot, such as important conversations, especially those that lead up to the climax or other key events. Don't waste space on descriptions or dialogue that don't move things along. But do leave in the parts that you think are important to the story.

Stretching a Story

Once in a while you might be asked to write as much as you can on a subject. It could be for a creative story or a report. This can be difficult because sometimes you don't have a whole lot of time to finish the assignment. With creative writing projects like this, most people just go with the first idea that pops into their head. That can lead to disaster. What I try to do is not think about when the paper is due, but think about the assignment itself. You might have an idea, but you have to make sure it's a subject you can write at length about.

Once you've picked a good idea, it's important to remember that, in this situation, filling space on the page is important. So get used to using lots of description and dialogue, which take up a lot of room. If you have to describe something, picture the setting in your head, then put it into words. Try not to use words that are too simple—instead of "pretty," use "stunningly beautiful" (longer). And instead of using "very," use "extremely." Not only do these descriptive words take up more space, they also make your story more interesting.

Bite into Those Boring Assignments

Let's face it, you're sometimes forced to write about something that puts you to sleep. Most of the time you can still squeeze your own interests into this kind of boring school assignment. I'm really into revolutionists, so my fictitious country report was all about how my island was started by slaves that were fed up with being pushed around by the British colonists. I made that assignment fun for me.

But be careful! Sometimes this can backfire on you. My friend was assigned to write a creative story with an Edgar Allen Poe theme. He went a little overboard with his own interests and forgot about the teacher's guidelines. Even though his story was well-written, he got a bad grade. Keep those guidelines in mind. But also remember, just because you get a bad grade on a story, that doesn't mean that it's *bad*. It just means it wasn't what the teacher wanted. I was so happy with my folk tale that I'm going back and writing it as it was meant to be—an epic.

Tips for Making Boring Assignments More Fun

1. When possible, write about things that interest you. The more you know about a subject, the more likely you are to get a better grade on the assignment. Plus, it makes the writing more fun for you.
2. Put your personality into the assignment. This is especially useful in reports. Don't write as if you are just recording information; write as if there is a person interviewing you on a particular subject.
3. Exchange ideas with friends. Sometimes listening to other people can inadvertently introduce new ideas from a simple conversation.

I hope my tips will help you see that writing doesn't have to be hard. You just have to get a good start and the story usually writes itself. Above all, don't get discouraged if you come up with mediocre stories. It happens to every writer—even the famous ones. Sometimes it's hard to keep an open mind, bounce back, and stay motivated. But don't give up. That's what creative writing is all about.

To learn more about writing, here are some books to read:

A Writer's Notebook by Ralph Fletcher

Edit Yourself by Bruce Ross-Larson

Scholastic Guides: Writing with Style by Sue Young

The Complete Guide to Writing Fiction by Barnaby Conrad

The Young Writer's Notebook by Susan and Stephen Tchudi

If you want to get some of your stories published, here are a few magazines to send your writing to (they publish stories written by kids):

Stone Soup: The Magazine by Young Writers and Artists
P.O. Box 83, Santa Cruz, CA 95063

Creative Kids: The National Voice for Kids
P.O. Box 8813, Waco, TX 76714-8813

Merlyn's Pen: The National Magazine for Student Writing
P.O. Box 1058, East Greenwich, RI 02818

SO, YOU WANNA BE A BLACK BELT?

Kris Stanley, age 10

✂ **Hobbies:** coin collecting ✎ **Favorite class:** math
📖 **Favorite book:** *The Lord of the Flies* ♫ **Hero:** Michael Jordan ❀ **Dream:** to be a police officer and work for the bomb squad

Zee Farrouge, age 12

✂ **Hobbies:** drawing, basketball, and playing the violin
✎ **Favorite class:** art ✐ **Favorite author:** Jules Verne
☹ **Pet peeve:** cracking my knuckles ♫ **Hero:** Michael Jordan
❀ **Dream:** to get drafted into the NBA and start my own animation company with the money I make

---

Martial Arts Glossary

Bo staff: A long wooden stick (five to six feet long) that is used to defend against other weapons.

Dan: There are nine degrees of black belts, called Dans, with first being the least difficult and ninth being the most difficult.

Dobok: A Tae Kwon Do uniform.

Dojang: A Tae Kwon Do school.

Gup: Any belt lower than black. There are nine Gup levels in Tae Kwon Do, from white to black stripe.

Hapkido: a martial art that focuses more on defense, uses more wrestling-like moves.

Hyung (or form): A series of Tae Kwon Do moves that lets you practice your skills against an imaginary opponent, using the same force you would in a real fight.

Master: You have to be at least a sixth Dan to be a Master.

Nunchukos: A weapon made of two short pieces of wood (each about a foot long) attached together by a short cord or chain.

Sparring: Mock-fighting for points. It is just like real fighting, but you don't touch your opponent.

Tae Kwon Do: Similar to karate, but more jumping and flying kicks and emphasis on mental and spiritual development.

Kris's Path to Black

In the beginning

I first found out about Tae Kwon Do in the summer of 1995. My dad signed me up for a three-week program in martial arts at a public school near my home. These first classes were taught by a second degree black belt. I liked it so much that when the session ended I signed up for another one. When the summer sessions ended, my instructor told me about the Dojang where he studied under the guidance of a sixth degree Master. My dad took me there to speak with Master Steven Bettencourt and signed me up to begin my studies.

My first test

I began, like everyone does, as a white belt. After many months, I took my first test and was promoted to ninth Gup. In the promotion I had to do a number of kicks and hand strikes, count in Korean, and show lots of other skills I had learned in my months of studies.

Since then, I've been promoted through all nine color belts, each with its own test and requirements. I progressed only when I proved myself and Master Bettencourt felt I was ready.

The proudest day of my life

Earlier this year, I was selected to take the test for promotion to first Dan. The black belt test is six hours long! I had to break boards with my hands and feet, demonstrate excellence in each Hyung, spar against three other black belt candidates at once, and perform all the required hand techniques, kicks, etc. At the end of the test, I was promoted to first Dan. Master Bettencourt tied my belt and presented me with my new Dobok. It was the proudest day of my life.

The pain

To be good at martial arts takes a lot of hard work. You have to practice a lot, be dedicated, and pay attention. I go to classes five or six days a week. My parents never have to make me go; I go because I want to. This year I even decided not to play baseball because the games conflicted with my Tae Kwon Do classes. I decided that baseball is something I would play for only a few more years, but I will have Tae Kwon Do forever.

And the glory

But it's easy to make the sacrifices because Tae Kwon Do is so fun. The more difficult the move is, the more I like learning it. The classes are great, especially sparring. We spar with each other in friendly competitions, get real sweaty, and have a lot of fun. Even though I'm just ten, I'm already qualified as an assistant instructor and get to help teach the lower ranking belts in the Gup classes.

I also take Hapkido lessons, which is fun because you learn to use your mental powers and to turn your opponent's force against him. I once saw a Hapkido Grand Master make his opponent feel numb all over just by staring at him!

But my favorite thing is the tournaments. So far, I've been in six Tae Kwon Do tournaments. In tournaments we're judged for our skills in Hyung, weapons (such as nunchukos and the Bo staff), board-breaking, and sparring. I've already won lots of trophies and medals, but the one I'm proudest of is a second place trophy for sparring. I won it in a Karate tournament even though I am a Tae Kwon Do student!

Why do I do it?

There are so many reasons why I love Tae Kwon Do:

☯ It has made me very strong, physically and mentally.

- I have the agility, strength, and self-confidence to know that I can defend myself if necessary. Tae Kwon Do teaches self-defense without aggression.

- I have learned a lot about self-control. The moves we practice could really hurt someone and I would only use them if I had to protect myself or someone else from serious harm.

- Some of my classes have both kids and adults in them, but age doesn't matter. The adults don't think of me as ten years old. In class we respect each other because we are the same: black belts. All the black belts are called "Mister" or "Missus," no matter how young or old they are. So I am called "Mr. Stanley."

- I am small in size but very big in my mind.

- It has given me inner peace. At the end of each class we meditate and practice breathing, which clears my mind. When I leave class I often feel like I'm getting a fresh start at life.

My martial arts future

I plan to continue studying under Master Bettencourt and to learn all he can teach me. My goal is to become a Master like he is and one day open my own school. I think by the time I start high school I will be a third Dan.

Becoming a black belt was the greatest thing I have ever done. It was a lot of very hard work but worth every minute. If I can do it, anyone can. If you're willing to work hard for your goal, you will feel really good about yourself when you do reach it.

Zee's Path to Black

How it all started

I first got interested in Tae Kwon Do when my mom told me about my uncle who is a well-respected Tae Kwon Do Master in Hawaii. Later we saw a parks and recreation pamphlet announcing after-school Tae Kwon Do classes. My brother and I took classes for six weeks and really got into it, so the instructor suggested we go to Master Bettencourt's Tae Kwon Do school. It was far from our house, but I really wanted to go.

Pop quiz!

The first day I went to the Dojang, I had to take a promotion test to go from white belt to ninth Gup. It was very stressful because it was my first test and I was terrified that I wouldn't pass. The judges asked me lots of questions and I had to do the white belt Hyung and lots of other stuff like sparring and even knife self-defense. Finally, when everyone was done testing, they presented me with my Gup belt. I passed the test!

Belts, belts, belts

After that, I took four to five classes a week and tested for belt after belt: yellow, white, yellow stripe, green stripe, green, blue stripe, blue, red stripe, red and black stripe. Ten belts in all!

The hardest belt

Eventually, it was time to test for my black belt. I was so excited. I prepared for three months and had to type a two-page essay about my life and take a written test. Then, after months of waiting, the day finally came. The test lasted six long hours and was the hardest thing I've ever done! But it was all worth it. I got my black belt with my name and my Dojang stitched on it. Now everyone in the Dojang calls me "Mr. Farrouge."

So much cool stuff

So far, I've been in five tournaments and have eight trophies and eleven medallions. I am very proud of all of them and I show them off to guests. Tournaments are fun, but sometimes they can be stressful. You have to go early in the morning and stay til late at night. I usually enter in the hyung, weapons (nunchukos), and sparring competitions. The top three competitors get trophies or gold, silver, and bronze medallions.

Tae Kwon Do got me interested in all kinds of martial arts. I'm now studying Hapkido as well. Hapkido has all sorts of wristlocks, takedowns, flips, and rolls. We learn how to defend ourselves with ease by redirecting our opponent's force away from us and also how to fall without hurting ourselves.

Weapons classes are also fun, learning how to use the nunchukos and the Bo staff. When I first started using nunchukos I had to use padded soft ones, but now that I am advanced and comfortable with them, I use the wooden ones. The Bo staff is five feet long and more difficult. It's pretty complicated and takes a lot of coordination.

Why do I do it?

What does martial arts mean to me? It's cool and makes me feel really good. It makes me feel strong and powerful. It means that I can walk through the halls of school without fear of being hurt or beaten up. Just knowing someone is a black belt is enough to make people think twice about fighting them. Even if I never have to use it, it still is comforting to know I could actually protect somebody's life (including my own).

Martial arts is not just about self-defense. It also helps me to mentally focus and concentrate on my goals in life. It helps me calm down when I am mad. When I practice I am able to release a lot of anger. Martial arts has made me stronger, not just physically, but mentally, as well. Since I started Tae Kwon Do I have had much better grades in school and I feel like I can do anything because I made black belt.

My martial arts future

I hope to advance in Tae Kwon Do. I am thinking about teaching some Tae Kwon Do classes when I'm older. Someday I might even become a Master.

Tae Kwon Do Tips

Q: What are the tournaments like?

A: Tournaments are usually held in school gyms and Tae Kwon Do schools from all over the state and surrounding states come to compete against one another in forms, weapons, sparring, demonstrations, and synchronized forms (when two or more students do the same form together). Trophies and medals are awarded to the best in each division and there's a grand champion trophy. Tournaments are long, hard, and stressful, but they're also very fun and exciting. Winning a trophy or medallion makes it worth the hard work and stress.

Q: Are the martial arts on TV and in the movies real?

A: You can tell that most of that stuff is fake and done by actors. Some of the moves look real, but if they actually hit each other like that they would be dead or seriously injured. They make it look like it doesn't hurt, but it does.

Q: What are some basic Tae Kwon Do moves?

A: Some of the first kicks are the side kick (using your heel), the front kick (using the ball of your foot), and the roundhouse kick (a sweeping kick that starts away from the body). The first punches you learn are the middle punch (aimed at the solar plexus) and the high punch (which is aimed between the upper lip and nose). Other moves you might learn are reverse punch, back fist, hammer fist, back kick, hook kick, crescent kick, single-jumping front kick, and flying side kick.

Q: Besides the moves, what will I learn from Tae Kwon Do?

A: You will learn:

- self-confidence and self-respect, which help you handle problems and conflicts without aggression.
- that you should never use violence unless it's your last choice.
- to be gentle to people younger than you and to respect your peers, your teachers, and even yourself.
- to trust people, even your opponents.

  The tenets of Tae Kwon Do keep us focused and calm our fears in the presence of an enemy. These tenets are:

  > *Courtesy:* Be polite and have good manners.
  > *Integrity:* Tell the truth.
  > *Perseverance:* Try your best and don't give up.
  > *Self-control:* Control your emotions.
  > *Indomitable spirit:* Have the courage to do what is right.

Q: What makes someone a Master?

A: Studying hard, dedicating your life to Tae Kwon Do, practicing all the time, teaching others, living your life in the way of the warrior. My instructor, Master Bettencourt, has been involved in Tae Kwon Do for thirty-five years.

Q: How can I get started?

A: Usually there are local schools or your city's parks and recreation department that support inexpensive classes. That's how lots of the kids in our Dojang got started. Look for Tae Kwon Do schools in the phone book under "Martial Arts," and if you can, check the Internet—some Dojangs have websites. When you find a school close by, visit and talk to the students before you sign up, to see how they like it. Also talk to the instructor and ask about his or her experience. Some Dojangs will even give a few free lessons so you can see if it's right for you.

DO YOU WANT TO BE AN AUTHOR TOO? HERE'S YOUR CHANCE

We will be publishing more *Boys Know It All* collections and are looking for more fantastic boy writers RIGHT NOW! If you are 6-16 years old and have a great chapter idea that isn't already in this book or is different in some way, you may be our next Boy Author!

Here are the rules:

1) Your chapter idea can be from you alone, or you can work together with your brother/s or best friend/s (they also have to be 6-16 years old).

2) Your chapter idea should be fun, unique, useful advice or activities for boys. It should also include one paragraph about why you chose to write about that topic or how you got your idea and why it's important or fun to you (if it's an activity).

3) Send us: 2-3 pages of your chapter idea, typed or clearly handwritten, 1 self-addressed stamped envelope (so we can send it back to you), and the *"Boys Know It All* Potential Author Questionnaire" (on next page, tear out).

4) You can also send us a photo of you if you want (any photo you like is fine with us). This is optional.

5) Send to: Boy Writer Contest
Beyond Words Publishing, Inc.
20827 N.W. Cornell Road, Suite 500
Hillsboro, Oregon 97124-9808

**Believe in yourself
Go for your dreams
We're waiting to hear from you!**

BOYS KNOW IT ALL
POTENTIAL AUTHOR QUESTIONNAIRE

Carefully **tear or cut out this page from your book** and fill out the following information in the space provided. Hand written is fine. If you can't think of an answer to something, it's okay to leave it blank. Then mail it to us with 2-3 pages of your chapter idea (see rules on previous page).

Name _____ **Age** _____

Address _____

City _____ **State** _____ **Zip** _____

Phone number (_____) _____

(So we can call you if you win. We won't call you for any other reason)

Your hobbies:

Your favorite subject or class in school:

Your favorite writer and/or book:

Your biggest pet peeve:

Your hero or role model:

Something that makes you unique:

Your dream:

Anything else you want to tell us:

OTHER GREAT BOOKS FROM
BEYOND WORDS PUBLISHING

So You Wanna Be a Rock Star:
Discover How to Play Music, Get Gigs, and Maybe Even Make It Big
Author: Stephen Anderson. $8.95, softcover. 120 pages.
A hip, how-to book that teaches young, aspiring musicians how to achieve their rock-and-roll dreams. The book begins with the basics, telling kids how to start their own bands with only their friends, a set of drums, and a lot of inspiration. In a fun yet informative style, Anderson teaches kids how to practice, get gigs in public, and maybe even become famous! Also profiles real kid bands who are out there playing and trying to get famous. Find out how *they're* doing it.

Better Than a Lemonade Stand: Small Business Ideas for Kids
Author: Daryl Bernstein. $8.95 softcover, $14.95 hardcover. 150 pages.
Written by a 15-year-old business guru who has been running his own businesses since he was eight, this book is for all you kid tycoons. It includes 51 kid-tested businesses you can start, plus how to advertise, expand, and keep customers happy.

"Dear Daryl, When I received your book, I came up with a great business idea and earned enough money to buy a laptop computer in one summer! Thanks!"—Brady, age 12

100 Excuses for Kids
Authors: Mike Joyer and Zach Robert. $5.95 softcover. 96 pages.
Two 9- and 10-year-old best friends have created a hysterical book that will give you great excuses for getting out of anything — vegetables, homework, chores . . . whatever!

Girls Know Best: Advice for Girls from Girls on Just About Everything
Authors: 26 girls $8.95 softcover. 160 pages.
The book that started it all. The first *Girls Know Best* contains great advice on everything from dealing with divorce to figuring out guys, and lots of fun chapters like how to play games in the sprinkler and tips for passing notes in class without getting caught. Everything you need to know, from the *real* experts!

Girls Who Rocked the World: Heroines from Sacagawea to Sheryl Swoopes
Author: Amelie Welden. $8.95 softcover. 120 pages.
Did you know that Joan of Arc was only 17 years old when she led French troops against armies of English invaders? Do you know about Cristen Powell, one of the top drag racers in the country, who began drag racing when she was just 16 years old? These are just a few of the amazing girls of the past and present who you will discover in this cool book. History isn't just about the guys anymore. Girls have rocked the world too!

To order any of these books or for a free catalog of all our books, call us at 1-800-284-9673 or e-mail us at info@beyondword.com.

Visit us on the world wide web! http://www.beyondword.com